A Time for Healing

A Time for Healing
Overcoming the Perils of Ministry

Jody Seymour

Judson Press ® Valley Forge

A Time for Healing: Overcoming the Perils of Ministry
© 1995, Judson Press, Valley Forge, PA 19482-0851

Bible quotations in this volume are from the New Revised Standard Version of the Bible, copyrighted 1989 by the Division of Christian Education of the National Council of the Churches of Christ in the United States of America, and are used by permission. All rights reserved. The Revised Standard Version of the Bible, copyright © 1946, 1952, 1971, by the Division of Christian Education of the National Council of the Churches of Christ in the U.S.A. and are used by permission.

Library of Congress Cataloging-in-Publication Data
Seymour, Jody, 1947-
  A time for healing : overcoming the perils of ministry / Jody
Seymour.
    p. cm.
  Includes bibliographical references.
  ISBN 0-8170-1235-4 (pbk. : alk. paper)
  1. Clergy—Mental health. 2. Clergy—Job stress. 3. Burn-out
(Psychology)—Religious aspects—Christianity. 4. Enneagram.
5. Clergy—Prayer-books and devotions—English. I. Title.
  BV4398.S48 1995
  253'.2—dc20   95-21708

Printed in the U.S.A.
97 98 99 00 01 02 8 7 6 5 4 3 2

To Betsy, my wife,
who has helped me overcome
some of the perils of ministry and
stood by me during the rest

Contents

Introduction. xii

Part I Biblical Models

Adam and Eve: You Can Run but You Can't Hide
The Humanness of Ministry 3

And Cain Killed Abel: Bloody Brothers
Ambition in Ministry 9

Jacob and Esau:
Would They Like Me If They Really Knew Me?
The Need for the Blessing. 14

King Saul: Still Crazy After All These Years
The Madness of Ministry. 18

David: The Man Who Would Be King
Clergy Sexual Misconduct 24

Jeremiah: Fire in the Belly but Ashes in the Soul
Clergy Burnout 31

Esther: You Mean My Preacher's a Woman?
The Wounds of Women in Ministry 36

Simon Peter:
If You Want to Walk on Water, First Have Breakfast with Jesus
Ministerial Effectiveness 40

Part II Using the Enneagram to Understand Ministerial Leadership Styles

The Enneagram Charts 49

Explanation of the Enneagram 54

The Nine Enneagram Types......................... 58

Type One: The Need to Be Perfect (The Perfectionist)
The Perfect Preacher 58

Type Two: The Need to Be Loved and to Love (The Helper)
The Sheltering Servant 59

Type Three: The Need to Succeed (The Achiever)
The Successful Shepherd.......................... 61

Type Four: The Need to Be Unique or Special (The Artist)
The Feeling Friend of Souls....................... 62

Type Five: The Need to Perceive (The Observer)
The Contemplative Creator 64

Type Six: The Need for Security (The Supporter)
The Church Cherisher............................. 65

Type Seven: The Need to Avoid Pain (The Optimist)
The Cheerful Charismatic......................... 67

Type Eight: The Need to Assert Oneself (The Leader)
The Powerful Prophet 68

Type Nine: The Need to Avoid Conflict (The Mediator)
The Peaceful Pastor.............................. 70

Enneagram Bibliography 72

Part III A Twenty-One-Day Spiritual Renewal Journey for Ministers

Introduction to the Journey 77
Day 1 Being a Child of God............................. 79
Day 2 Come As a Child 80
Day 3 Coming Home 81
Day 4 The Knowledge of God 82
Day 5 The Call to Ministry 83
Day 6 Resistance to the Call 84
Day 7 Sabbath 85

Day 8 Remembering Your Mother: The Church 86
Day 9 Testing the Spirits. 87
Day 10 Bread for the Journey. 88
Day 11 Education for Ministry. 89
Day 12 Temptations 90
Day 13 Water into Wine: Remembering Success. 91
Day 14 Facing Fear with Jesus 92
Day 15 Remembering Your Power 93
Day 16 Remembering a Misuse of Power 94
Day 17 The Need for Forgiveness 95
Day 18 The Wounds of Ministry 96
Day 19 A Time for Healing 97
Day 20 The Need for Renewal 99
Day 21 A Revisioning of Ministry 101
Conclusion. 103
Notes 107

Acknowledgments

I would like to acknowledge the Graduate Theological Foundation in Donaldson, Indiana, for their support in allowing me to use the work on this book as part of their degree program. I would also like to thank the many ministers who have participated in the renewal retreats that I have helped lead. Those brothers and sisters on the journey have helped me as much as I have helped them.

Introduction

The seeds for this book were planted a few years ago as I found myself standing in front of a microphone at the executive session of our Annual United Methodist Conference. My eyes were moist, and my throat was dry.

This was not a time for impassioned speeches. The ministers who had gathered were there for the purpose of routinely voting on new candidates for ministry and other related matters dealing with "ministerial connection" (that is, who will remain in the ministry and who will not).

We had just voted on those who would be placed on leave of absence, involuntary location, or who had surrendered their ministerial credentials. I knew the circumstances of some of these people. I stood at the microphone because a sharp pain had pierced my sense of the routine and said something like the following:

Bishop, each year we come to this place and begin our session by standing to honor those of our number who have died. It is appropriate that we honor them, but there are others of our number who are experiencing a different kind of death. We quickly vote on them and pass on. These are ministers who have died to ministry because of different kinds of brokenness. They are the wounded whom we allow to die quietly while they somehow still live. They are casualties. When are we going to do something about this? How many other names are going to be read into our records before we start paying attention to our need for healing?

I sat down in the midst of a strange silence, a silence of consent. Too many of my clergy brothers and sisters knew about the subject of my babbling. The pain of which I spoke came from the story of the minister who became involved with another woman. The walking death related to the minister whose sexual orientation was called into question. I was speaking of the ones called of God who had cracked under the pressure of the competitive system.

In the ranks of the wounded were those who had lost their souls at the altar of success and image. I was tired of the lists. It was time to proclaim that the "emperor was naked" and that *we* were the emperor.

Our bishop acknowledged the need for something to happen. Later, many of those who had earlier filled the silence of the room encouraged me to do something. What I did was write some legislation, which when passed provided for fifteen "healing pastors" to be trained who would stand with those who were experiencing transition in ministry. Along with these efforts to support healing was the setting up of a yearly program in which ministers in their fifth and fifteenth years of ministry would be required to attend a three-day renewal retreat. The required nature of the retreats was written in because too many ministers are like me; they would not go unless it was required.

It was time for some grace to be legislated alongside some of our rules. The number of the wounded who had fallen under the yoke were too numerous to ignore. It was time for healing.

The book you now hold in your hands is my response to the pain I feel. The pain comes from some of my own hurt encountered while attempting to be human and be a minister. The pain also comes from listening too long to lists of those in ministry who have become the walking dead.

Ministers are wounded because they are human. In this book I point out some of the unique pitfalls in ministry that cause conflict and pain. God's representatives have some unique vulnerabilities.

I am tired of the "elder brother" syndrome, which is typical of the gathered clergy as one of our wounded is discussed. It is time for healing. It is time to examine some of the reasons for our pain.

This book is not just another effort to document the causes of ministerial woundedness. What I desire to do is hold up some of our wounds to the light of the story that ministers know best, the narrative of Scripture. The Scripture is not only the story that ministers weekly convey to their people; it is also *our* story.

It is time to look in the mirror and see not only the person of the cloth, but to also see the "shadow" that comes with that very human person. As John Sanford has said,

> Without a connection to our dark inner personality we are not real; we are not a solid personality, and cannot be seen for who we are.
> The ministering person is tempted to try to live without a Shadow, and others will unwittingly assist in this devilish business because they do not want to see the ministering person's Shadow either; they want that person to stand only in the light and not have any darkness.[1]

The darkness is real. The shadow needs to be seen for what it is: a source of power and pain. It is time to remember *our* stories and *the* story. The two are powerfully connected, just as humanness is connected to ministry.

The first part of this book relates the biblical story to various types of ministerial woundedness. The second section uses the Enneagram to shed light on ministerial leadership styles to help the minister better understand the unique ways that individual wounds happen. The Enneagram is an ancient tool for self-understanding. I have used it for my own spiritual formation and have found it most helpful in leading others to a better self-understanding as they prepare for their continuing spiritual journeys.

Since this book is primarily designed for the minister, the third part of the text is a twenty-one-day, self-guided journey of renewal. This journey is offered to assist the minister in his or her examination of life and ministry. The journey uses Scripture, guided meditation, and the recalling of past episodes to help the pilgrim look again at the signs that have been there along the way.

This book is part of my own healing. I have discovered that to share myself is to see myself. Thus far I have survived ministry. This book is an offering to those, and there are many, who are in the struggle to survive and keep their humanity intact.

It is time for healing. It is time to rediscover who we are in light of God's calling and God's grace.

PART I

BIBLICAL MODELS

The Humanness of Ministry

All who have been ordained have heard it. It is meant to be a kind of strange compliment. The words are intended to give a sense of ease and permission. They are words that allow persons of the cloth to become part of the human enterprise. The words are: "Well, ministers are human, too."

If the unordained knew how truly human those of us who are "set aside" really are, it would scare them. The truth is that many who enter ministry are very needy people. This does not mean that those of us in ministry should not be ministers, but it does mean that we should be honest about our needs or we will end up in trouble.

> One study of the ministerial personality points out the reality of the neediness of persons in ministry: "Ministers tended to be more guilt-ridden, anxious, self-punishing in the face of hostility and aggression, more insecure, defensive, passive, conforming, dependent, rebellious, and idealistic than other people."[1]

Just reading the above list can make one tired. Scratch below the surface and the discovery is made that not only are ministers human, they are *very* human.

The first issue to face in delving into ministerial woundedness is ministerial humanness. Every helping profession needs to embrace the reality that those who try to help are often acting out their own need to be helped. This reality should not be shocking, but it is often overlooked. The truth of this observa-

3

tion can be a source of power rather than a source of woundedness if it is properly faced and embraced.

Alan Jones, in his book *Sacrifice and Delight: Spirituality for Ministry*, describes the need for those in ministry to embrace their humanness: "The primary vocation of ministers with regard to their sense of self is to be earthed, to be as humanly human as they know how. We are called to help people find their way home, and we cannot do this unless we are at home with ourselves."[2]

Much of the pain in ministry is caused by the unwillingness or inability to face a human, interpersonal need. Somehow ministers think that they can skip over these needs and go on to help others. But it only takes a brief look at psychological dynamics to see the danger involved in overlooking personal needs. The neglected human need of the minister is transferred onto the persons and congregations who are being served. Combine this with the transference that occurs in the other direction, from the congregation and individual church members toward the minister, and the result is either ego inflation or weariness.

The transference can at first feel good to the minister who needs to be stroked, but it can quickly turn to weariness. John Sanford points this out:

> To carry a transference means that something has been handed to us that we are expected to live up to. It also means that if our all-too-human reality should break through and disrupt the transference, the person will see us in terms of a negative transference instead, and it is no fun to carry a negative transference for someone. Most of all, it wearies us to carry a transference because we are essentially carrying some of the psyche of other people that they need to find within themselves.[3]

Transference works both ways, and either direction has its dangers.

Sometimes the unrecognized need is sublimated. In these cases, the need is acted out through inappropriate behavior, such as sexual misconduct, overwork, and burnout. There are many clinical studies that document such transference and acting out.

What I wish to do is relate the needs of ministers to the story most familiar to us, the biblical narrative. For many ministers, the relating of the biblical narrative to people's lives is an every Sunday occurrence. However, it is time for ministers to spend more time seeing where we are in that same story.

It Started in the Beginning

There is no need to spend time documenting that the Adam and Eve story is mythologically true rather than factually true. This realization points to the story's human truth. People like Joseph Campbell have shown how myth points to a deeper truth than fact.[4]

Adam and Eve forgot who they were. Ministers do the same. Because the minister thinks that he or she is "set apart," there is a dangerous, though subtle, separation from the human family and its "mess."

Ministers should remember that those who are called to name the demons are in danger of being captured by them. Eugene Peterson reminds those who would name the spirits that

I have not yet seen statistics on the shipwrecks of those who speak and act in Jesus' name in this pain- and sin-stormed world, . . . but the numbers, if we had access to them, would most certainly both stagger and sober us. The moment any of us embarks on work that deals with our fellow humans at the core and depths of being where God and sin and holiness are at issue, we become at that same moment subject to countless dangers, interferences, pretenses, and errors that we would have been quite safe from otherwise. So-called "spiritual work" exposes us to spiritual sins. Temptations of the flesh, difficult as they are to resist, are at least easy to detect. Temptations of the spirit usually show up disguised as invitations to virtue.[5]

The Adam and Eve story, though too familiar to most clergy, is a perfect example of being captured. The picture of those first two persons who were called by God has become for ministers like a painting hanging in the hallway that is passed by but unnoticed.

We ministers have the "sin of Adam" within us in more ways

than one. Perhaps we think that in dealing with godly things, we are exempt from such familiar, human traps. Just writing these words makes me realize how foolish such thoughts are, but we do have them. The office of minister gets to us without us knowing it. Someone needs to be around to tell us that we are "naked." "Hey Adam, hey Eve, look in the mirror. Remember who you are."

Oftentimes when I am with a group of ministers in an official setting, I am amazed at how unhuman we act. We cloak ourselves in all kinds of religious or ecclesiastical verbiage in an effort to sew together fig leaves. I vacillate on these occasions between being amused and disheartened.

Most ministerial gatherings need someone who could function as the "court fool." The fool's function would be to add disclaimers when perspective is lost. So much of what ministers do when we gather is silly. We are afraid of our humanness.

Perhaps rather than a court fool being present, the searching voice of God could be heard saying, "Adam...Eve, where are you?"

God tried to tell those early ancestors of ours that being human was enough. The agenda was full. It seems that we did not need to be more than human. Being more than human leads to being less than human.

For ministers, the snake in the tree has many names. The generic name that best fits is "Power Hidden in Humility." This may sound like *Dances with Wolves*, but so be it. The biblical precedent has been set by the names poor old Hosea had to give his children: Not Pitied, Not My Child.

Being human is the major ingredient of being a good minister. If this is true, then ministers need to work on human gifts *and* human weaknesses. To overdo the gifts or deny the weaknesses is to place oneself in the middle of the original-sin camp.

The biblical story tries to convey to the minister that all are godlike because all are human. We are not godlike when we try to be God. God is the only one without needs. Creatures of the dust have needs and need to admit it.

God originally said, "You need to allow me to be me and not what you want me to be. You need each other. You need to be honest with each other. You need to be mindful of your limitations." And after we did not pay attention to the above, God clearly said, "You need to remember that you have messed up and are in constant need of me."

The question for the minister is the question asked by God in the garden that cool evening long ago: "Where are you?" The ordained person cannot hide behind the call, the robes, or the work. Like the human family whom ministers are called to serve, needs must be dealt with or they will deal with the minister.

It is good to remember that the Adam and Eve story was written after the fact. People who wrestled with why they were the way they were wrote this story to help explain how God could have let the human family get in the shape it was in. Those ancient Hebrew seekers knew that they were outside the garden. They simply tried to document why.

Ministers hear God's call through human needs, not in spite of those needs. If God is God, then God knows what God is doing when we are called. God knew the Adam- and Eve-like dust that would one day be covered over by collar or robe. God needs ministers to not hide behind needs but to try to understand those needs.

Given what ministers are called to do, it is a crime that we are not required to do more work on our own internal framework. Many ministers are guilty of malpractice because they have never practiced on themselves. They need help.

Good, solid clinical pastoral education and the accompanying supervision should be required of all those who attempt to respond to the call to be ministers. Such a relationship to persons who are helping us see ourselves will help us to stay healthy and open.

So many times we are excused from such evaluation because of our "holy work." Somehow it is assumed that we are above such human needs. Wrong. If you are a minister and are reading these words, you know how "unabove" we really are. Who are we kidding?

After working with countless ministers, Alan Jones has surmised that ministers are the most reluctant group to do self-examination and spiritual journeying.[6] I agree.

It is time to quit hiding. It is time to realize and embrace our conversations with the voices that come from trees. It is time to look at what fig leaves we have selected.

This self-examination is not for the purpose of shaming but for the purpose of being honestly human. That is what living outside the garden means. Ministers do not preach to their people from somewhere in the garden. We are with them, east of Eden. We know it, and they need to know it. We do not have to strip naked in front of the people we serve. That is inappropriate. But we must join them as people who are aware of the human condition.

Our family tree as ministers has the names Adam and Eve clearly marked. Ministerial woundedness often has its origin in not remembering this original reality.

Ambition in Ministry

It used to be called "the brotherhood" until women entered the ministry. Now it is often referred to as "the covenant community." The problem is that the collection of professionals called ministers is often neither covenantal nor community. When two or more ministers gather together, both competition and collective ambition are present.

Ambition in ministry is often hidden. Ministers are not supposed to fall victim to the sin of professionalism. Many ministers are, however, type-A personalities who are still trying to prove something. This phenomenon is not all bad since it can be the source of great energy and effort. What must be remembered is the insight offered long ago, which supposedly came from the Sufi tradition: Too much of a good thing is a bad thing.

If ambition is a source of clergy power, it must be recognized for what it is, or it could play itself out in some very destructive ways. Wanting to do a good job and getting ahead are not bad things.

I have heard too many pep talks from those in leadership positions who have climbed up the professional ladder of ministry reminding the ministerial community of the dangers of professionalism. Ministers are often scolded for forgetting their high calling with such language as, "You are called to be servants of Christ, not religious professionals."

Listening to such words reminds me of the doctor who talks with the patient about how bad smoking is for health and then walks out of the room to light up a cigarette. How did those who lecture to us get to be where they are? It is easy to talk about diets when one is full and satisfied.

Clergypersons would be healthier if we faced up to our ambition, named it, and claimed it. Knowing what confession means, it would be appropriate to admit our jealousy of one another. Perhaps if we confessed our personal ambitions and envy, we could go on to some renewal of a true covenant community relationship.

Ministers can become like Cain standing behind a tree, trying to wash his bloody hands as God says, "Hey, Cain, where is that brother of yours?" "Go ask him yourself; he's not my responsibility" was just another way of saying "Not me; I'm not guilty."

The truth is that many clergy are jealous of those who "make it." In most denominations, there exists a pyramid system, with the majority of churches being small. As one moves toward the top of the pyramid, there are fewer places to go. The air gets thin at the top. Not everyone can be there, even if he or she desires such a lofty place.

The ways of getting there can be bloody. When one of the brothers gets in trouble or does a terrible job, there should be no joy in Zion. The sad truth is that often there are hidden smiles among the faithful because this means that one less person will be jockeying for position at the peak of things.

I do not mean to sound bitter about this situation. I am not bitter, but it could be because I have been able to achieve a certain level of success. I have listened to the rumblings from the community as I journeyed. If I choose to be honest, I have contributed to some of those rumblings.

Our shadow side comes out when those of our number are wounded. We need to face this shadow if there is to be any sense of true community. When the shadow of ambition is not faced, it comes out in various projections.

Thomas Maeder has described what can happen to those in helping professions when the shadow is not faced:

> The danger occurs when the wounded healer has not resolved or cannot control his own injury. The helping professional's career can follow either of two paths. The more difficult, but ultimately more satisfying, road leads to a painful confrontation with his own problems and weaknesses,

and ultimately to self-knowledge. Ideally, he overcomes the difficulties; at worst, he is forced to resign himself to insuperable handicaps. In either case, though, the end result is a clearer perception of his ambitions and needs and their relationship to the task at hand. He can approach others with honesty, compassion, and humility, knowing that he is motivated by genuine concern, and not by some ulterior motive.

The other path is easier and often disastrous. The [minister] comes, consciously or unconsciously, to see in his profession a means of *avoiding* the need to deal with his problems. He gains authority and power to compensate for his weakness and vulnerability. He learns slippery techniques that enable him to justify his actions in almost all circumstances.[1]

We ministers kill each other tenderly with our game of pretend. Desire to be above someone else must be acknowledged or it can have destructive consequences. Ask Cain.

Why could Cain not have worked through his less-than-blessed status? His ability was not rewarded at first. God said basically, "Hang on and do not let your lesser sacrifice be the cause of sin." God was suggesting that Cain was going to have to put up with some unfairness and then hope that God would still be God.

Cain's timetable did not allow for such patience. He took things into his own hands and made sure that the standard for comparison would be leveled out by his elimination of the standard. He killed the comparison. It did not work then, and it does not work now.

We clergy do not put out contracts on our brothers and sisters in the ministry, but some might as well. I am reminded of the cartoon that depicts two very lean vultures perched in a tree. One vulture looks to the other and says, "Patience my ass, I'm going to kill something." Maybe every clergyperson needs this cartoon somewhere in the office as a reminder of what the hunger of untamed ambition can do. The shadow is sometimes vulture-like.

When clergy perceive that other brothers or sisters have the "blessing," a dangerous climate is created. If this is mixed with certain unmet needs from childhood, the need to prove oneself becomes the basis for envy and unhealthy comparisons. The

choice is either to work on oneself or psychologically attack
other persons who become the object of projections.

The key to overcoming such unhealthy comparisons is nothing new. There are many books available about the need for
spiritual renewal for those called to ministry. We must return to
our center or we will be out of balance. The potter's wheel is a
good symbol for such uncenteredness. Once we are not centered
the result will always be lopsided.

Another problem is that the "rewards" for clergy are often
unclear. Ministers do not know what success is except for the
standards that are often set by the institution. The church-
growth movement, fueled by institutional-survival fear, has
added to this dilemma.

Ambition can turn to sin when the measurement for success
(which will be discussed in a subsequent chapter) gets out of
balance. So often numbers and the drive to become a larger
church are the measurements for success in ministry. Eugene
Peterson has asked if such "successful leadership" is

> inspired by the Holy Spirit or a boastful arrogance fed by an
> anxious ego? Is this assertive leadership courageous faith or
> self-importance? Is this suddenly prominent preacher with a
> large and admiring following a spiritual descendant of Peter
> with five thousand repentant converts or of Aaron indulging
> his tens of thousands with religious song and dance around
> the golden calf?[2]

Ecclesiastical leaders who are constantly encouraging their
ministers to increase the flock need to be mindful of the fields
upon which they are casting the seed. Some fields will not
produce much yield in terms of numbers. Other measures for
success need to be held up as ways of measuring faithfulness in
ministry. If size becomes an idol, then we should not be sur-
prised that the Cain story repeats itself within the ministry.

Many clergy have been parented in a climate that has con-
vinced them that big is beautiful and that hard work should
produce a shiny product. Good things do happen in big, successful churches, but since all clergy cannot serve such churches,
we need to quit setting ministers up for failure.

Malony and Hunt, in their book *The Psychology of Clergy*, offer
a different model for judging clergy effectiveness by focusing

on changed insights and understandings as the primary meas-urement. They refer to research done by Burley Howe, which states that effectiveness should be defined "in terms of having effect on those ministered to." The study goes on to show how the model of a physician's practice is one way to view this:

> The only appropriate measure of physicians' success is whether their patients get well, not the size of their practices, the elegance of their offices, their bedside manners, or their sophisticated knowledge about medical literature. These ac-tivities are instrumental means to an end but not the primary goal. Likewise with ministers. Task performance and per-sonal attractiveness are means to an end: the changed identity and altered life-perception of people resulting from changes in insights and understandings.[3]

Cain killed Abel because Cain was using the wrong measur-ing stick for his own identity. The secret was not the sacrifice that was brought to the altar but the heart and attitude of the one approaching the altar.

Those of us who spend a lot of time around altars ought to know better, but we are human before we are clergy. A bishop once told a group of male clergy that they were being ordained because God did not trust them to be laypersons.[4]

The blood on the priest's hands should be from the sacrifice offered for the people and not from the results of butchering each other on the altar of ambition. This butchering will con-tinue if we are not honest and if we are not careful with the measurements we use for effectiveness and success.

We need to look in the mirror and see the mark of Cain. It is the beginning of our healing.

The Need for the Blessing

The day is still very vivid in my memory. I was in the middle of a clinical pastoral education (CPE) unit. My supervisor was questioning me about one of my verbatims. (A verbatim is a written version of a conversation between a client and a patient or, in this case, between a pastor and parishioner.) This particular verbatim was centered on a hospital visit with a woman who was dying of cancer. She had been "dying" for over a year. Her husband was one of the leaders in the small, rural, family church that I was serving at the time.

My three years at this church had been difficult. I was a young preacher who had mistakenly thought he could change those people in that church. I was the young preacher who, according to them, was just "passing through." As one of the brothers from one of the dominant families had been heard to say, "This preacher is too young, too little, and he's read too many books."

To say that I was having trouble with being accepted was putting it mildly. I was miserable. On many occasions I had entertained the idea of leaving the ministry. The four years I stayed there were long, but I know now that they were needed. I realize now that much of my reasoning revolved around some personal needs to be accepted and loved. I needed that love and acceptance too much.

The verbatim consisted of my recounting of an afternoon visit to Catherine's hospital room. She was experiencing morphine-induced mood swings. It had been a long battle. She needed to die.

It had also been a long battle for her husband, Ralph. Ralph was another one of "the brothers." He was also the church lay leader. Whenever Ralph had the opportunity, he would tell me how my preaching just was not reaching the mark. I was not "hard enough" on the people. "People do not need to hear how good they are," he would say sternly. "They need to be reminded of how bad they are."

In his own way, Ralph tried to be tolerant of me. I could tell that, though it was a strain for him, he tried to be patient with me. I would learn when I got older, he would say.

Then it happened. It was just a sentence, but somehow it must have broken through to my soul. As we stood beside Catherine's groaning body, Ralph began to tell me about "some preacher" who had come by the room the day before, offering to pray for Catherine's healing. Hearing Ralph describe who this preacher was and what kind of church he served, I knew that this preacher was closer to Ralph's theological bent than I would ever be. As Ralph continued the story, he stopped and looked at me, as if waiting for me to ask a question. I simply asked, "What did you say to him, Ralph?" Ralph said, "I told him I already had a preacher."

This sounds like a simple enough statement when it is written out on a piece of paper for a required verbatim. But as I recounted it verbally to my supervisor, my eyes filled with tears. I had to stop. My next words were broken with sobs. I did not understand what was happening.

In typical CPE style, the supervisor allowed me some time to cry. There was some needed silence, followed by his question, "What do you think the tears mean?" I had no answer except to say that I did not understand the intensity of my feelings.

Then he said, "Do you think perhaps that you needed a blessing from Ralph?" Ah, the blessing. My supervisor then helped me explore my need for affirmation and blessing. I became freer on that afternoon because the passion behind my need became evident for the first time. I needed the blessing.

Many people in ministry need this blessing. It is one of the reasons that people enter ministry. Studies have shown that many who choose the ministry have a clear need for affirmation and nurture.[1] There is nothing wrong with this reality *if* it is recognized.

The people at that small, rural church could not meet all of

my needs for affirmation. They were not even good at affirming
each other. The giving of affirmation was not a part of their
subculture. To most of them, the giving of affirmation implied
some kind of weakness.

Too much of my emotional energy was given away trying to
win their affirmation, their blessing. My purchase of a CB radio
was one example. I hated CB radios, but everyone else in the
community had one, so I put one in my car. I even was bestowed
a handle (one's CB call name). "Hey, Rabbi, got your ears on?"
I know now that they must have laughed at my efforts to fit in.
My need for individuation was not going to be met by a swish-
ing antenna and a new name.

All people need blessing. Wanting the blessing too much is
one avenue toward unhappiness. The story of Jacob and Esau
in Genesis 27 reminds the reader of both how important the
blessing is and how dangerous not being honest about it can be.

To what lengths do ministers go to get the blessing? Like
Jacob, some of us become someone we are not in order to get the
blessing. We wear all kinds of emotional skins, like our faith
ancestor Jacob, in order to obtain the blessing. If we get the
blessing by making others blind to our real selves, we end up
with an empty blessing.

Blessing is always grounded in grace. The blessing must be
given, not awarded. Popularity may seem like the blessing, but
if it is gained at too high an emotional price, it actually becomes
a curse. Like Jacob, ministers find that they have to go to all sorts
of lengths to maintain the blessing.

John Sanford points to the problem with being who we are
not:

> We can strike a pose and seem to be [a certain] way, but if it
> is not what we genuinely are and feel at the time, we are not
> real but something of a fake. . . . We will lose touch with our
> genuine self if we try to be something we are not. . . . [This
> will] exhaust us, because it takes energy to pretend to be
> something we are not, but will also impoverish our person-
> ality, and, in the long run, also impoverish our congregation.[2]

Ursula Le Guin portrays this same reality in her fantasy
entitled *A Wizard of Earthsea*. In this story, a young boy is taught
the craft of wizardry by a wise, old wizard. Within the story is

the caution to the young lad, who has turned himself into a hawk in order to fight the great dragon, that he cannot remain something he is not for too long or it will destroy him.[3]

Like the young lad in Le Guin's story, ministers often try to fly where we need not go. Not only is it emotionally dangerous, it is not helpful in the long run.

The blessing needs to come from being who we really are. If the blessing is not there to be had, then we need to be psychologically strong enough and integrated enough to maintain ego integrity in times of no blessing.

Alan Jones reminds us that the ministry contains more than its share of emotionally unstable persons. He goes on to state that this should not be so surprising, since ministers, like other helping professionals, tend to go into the nurturing vocations because of the need to be nurtured. What is surprising, Jones writes, is their "unwillingness to name [the pathology] and face it. . . . There seems to be a gospel—good news—for everyone except the clergy." Many clergy have hurried childhoods and grow up quickly. They become healers, "believing that hard work and responsibility are the only things that give them value in other's eyes."[4]

Somewhere along the line of self-examination, ministers must face their need for the blessing. Some of us may not have received the blessing as children. If we did not receive this blessing, we might spend our lives and our work trying to get it.

This search is not fair to the churches we serve, nor is it healthy for the minister. Blessings are better received when we quit desperately looking for them. Jacob had to return to the place of his manipulation in order to finally receive a real blessing. He was simply looking for healing and wholeness with his brother. What Jacob received was blessing.

In the next section of this book, the Enneagram will be offered as one way to take this pilgrimage toward self-discovery. As we journey toward our true selves, we are given the opportunity to discover where along the path we needed blessing. This journey, when blended with the accepting grace of God, can lead to the blessing needed most: the blessing of oneself.

The Madness of Ministry

A minister writes the following about the ministry: "Many believe God must have been mad to have called *us*. There are times when we believe we must have been mad to accept. The madness of the call is that it most often takes us along paths we do not prefer, and assigns duties for which we feel most ill-equipped."[1]

King Saul is a prime example of the madness that accompanies the divine call. Saul was not looking to be king. The story in 1 Samuel 9–10 recounts that Saul was simply looking for his father's asses when he was picked to be king. The cynic might say that Saul did not find his father's asses but became one himself.

The divine call can make many things of us, and yes, being somewhat of an "ass" can be one of them. The divine call can make ministers assume jobs and roles that they are ill equipped to handle. The call was and is supposed to be a rather dangerous mantle to wear.

To do God's bidding is an awesome thing. We are dealing with things that are almost impossible to handle. If the Word of God does not consume us, the people of God might. Between the expectations of the divine office and the demands of the people we serve, emotional weariness can weigh us down.

The story of Saul seems cruel at first reading. A man attempted to lead the people for God and suddenly was told that the young punk down the block who did not even have a seminary education had been selected by God to be the new king.

When Saul inquired of Samuel as to why such a thing had happened, Saul was told that the Lord had withdrawn his favor from Saul. The fine print in 1 Samuel 15:15 indicates that the transgression that caused this rebuke was the fact that Saul had not "utterly destroyed" all the men, women, infants, ox and sheep, camels and asses of the Amalekites.

After putting on some Old Testament glasses of interpretation, the point of the story was that God's blessing had left Saul because he had not been obedient to the company line. Obedience was and is important to the "boss." Obedience represents who is in charge. Obedience is also a reflection of integrity, for even if no one else knows, God knows.

First Samuel 18:10 says that Saul ended up raving within his house. Many ministers can empathize with poor old Saul. Ministers suffer from many kinds of madness. Clergy depression is common. So many times we who are charged with the healing of souls get on with the business without tending to our own healing.

Being "less than whole" does not mean that ministers cannot function effectively. There does need to be an awareness of this less-than-whole status so that needed work can be done for oneself. If we fake it for too long and act as if we are whole, we can end up depressed or resentful of our people, the ministry, and maybe God. John Sanford has described what can happen:

> Since the ministering person functions in a role in which [he or] she is handed a persona by the persons [he or] she serves, [the minister] is in danger of losing [a sense of self]. But if we lose ourselves, we will also lose our energy. We will become like a watch that has lost its mainspring because we will have lost contact with our genuine Self, the Center of our being. . . . Meanwhile, the real energy of the personality will accumulate in the unconscious, activating the Shadow, and setting up a state of inner opposition to an Ego that is so identified with the persona that it is becoming increasingly two-dimensional and stale. The result will be anxiety, despondency, and lack of creativity.[2]

Such dryness along the pilgrimage of ministry can lead the minister to the same place that Saul found himself. Saul ended up consulting a source other than God for the soothing of his anxiety, despondency, and lack of creativity. Saul spoke with the witch of Endor because "the LORD did not answer him either by dreams. . . or by prophets" (1 Samuel 28:6).[3]

There are not many voices out there to whom ministers can turn when they feel on the outs with God. We cannot share our predicament because the people we serve assume that we would never experience such dryness of our souls. There is a madness to this dilemma. We need good counsel. There is a need to share the dryness with someone who will listen. We want that old experience of God again, that experience that surrounded us when we were fresh with our call. But it may not be there.

There has been an erosion of faith. We think we have to hide this. Our people must not know. This hiding becomes a tremendous burden. While carrying this burden, many a minister has sought his or her own "witch of Endor." I recently worked with a minister who reached out in his dryness to find some comfort. He found himself in an entrapment situation on a street corner as a prostitute offered her services. He was empty and dry; he needed some water. Like the person in a lifeboat who will drink the ocean salt water even though that water will eventually kill the one who drinks it, this minister took a drink.

The press loved it because, not only was the water poison, the woman was a police officer. It was like a feeding frenzy. In one moment this man lost his job, many of his friends, his home, and potentially his future.

As I listened to his story, I heard the recounting of the hazards of ministry. He was on that street corner because he was lost— not lost spatially, but lost emotionally. Who was he to consult? This minister needed a strong yet gentle mentor to help him find some water on the journey. He found a witch.

He was later diagnosed as being clinically depressed, but the press did not print this fact. The press did not care to explain *why* he was on that street corner. The press simply did not care. The story was simple: the surgeon had dirty hands.

I hoped that this minister's congregation would care, but structures and rules made it hard for the church to care. Procedures had to be followed that, although they were designed for healing, actually prevented the people in the church who wanted to care for this broken pastor from doing so.

The dual-role nature of ministry has been studied by

researchers and found to be a unique burden within ministry. Dual-role relationships are defined as "those in which people play several different roles with those they serve." In other words, clergy "interact with parishioners in a variety of settings."[4] It is hard to ask for help from those you are supposed to be helping. The minister is supposed to be the strong, spiritual leader. How can the leader lead if he or she is lost? So we hide our times of lostness. In so doing, we sometimes seek out "witches." When we do, we do a disservice to our people because they could learn from the appropriate sharing of our dryness.

The list of ministers who have "fallen on their own swords" is much too long. Some have literally taken their own lives, but many more have destroyed their lives in ministry by seeking out witches. If they are caught, they pay. Even if they are not caught, they end up being drained because of the energy it takes to cover up the places where they drank from poisoned water.

No other profession has the constancy of this dual-role hazard. We are entangled with the people we serve. These entanglements can be wonderful if responsible friendship can evolve from them, but they are often problematic because of the reality of "Who will serve the server?"

It should be required that ministers have a person or a group who will help them with this ever-present potential crisis. If that group cannot be a small, trusted group within the church, the minister needs to find a person or group outside the church.

Ministers also need to remember that the dry times are a part of any spiritual journey. We almost need a spiritual circuit breaker that warns us when we get to a certain level of dryness, a warning light if you will. Often another person or a group will recognize this reality before we do.

Eugene Peterson discovered this reality in his own ministry. He compared the journey to mountain climbing:

> Most experienced climbers, faced with a high and difficult mountain, rope themselves together for their ascent. There is a skilled lead climber; if someone falls there is a linked safety system. But some climbers set out on their own. They bush-whack through the underbrush, laboriously figure out each difficulty on the mountain with guidebook, map, compass,

and a lot of trial and error. These climbers also gain the summit, but the accidents and fatalities among them are far more frequent. On the lower slopes of the mountain, it never occurred to me to have a guide. But about halfway up the mountain, alarmed at how many maimed and dead bodies of other pastors I was seeing, I became frightened. Aware of the danger of the enterprise and my own ignorance of the mountain, I decided that I must have a skilled guide, a spiritual director.[5]

Somewhere, halfway up the mountain, ministers may opt to fall on their own swords because they do not see the options for guidance around them. There is too much madness in ministry to take the journey alone. When we think that God is not there, the aloneness can be unbearable. We seek out all sorts of salves for our pain.

God *is* there, but who tells the thirsty minister that? It is time to announce, at least to each other, that we need help. If this is overheard by the people we serve, so be it. I would rather disappoint them with honesty than have them judge me for consulting a witch.

Our madness is our gift. The divine call is real, but it has always had within it an element of madness. Our people may not understand this, for they somehow think that we have been privileged to see God face-to-face.

What the people we serve need to remember is what Moses discovered when he wanted to see God face-to-face. Moses was told by the Almighty that he could not handle God face-to-face. It would be enough for Moses to catch sight of God's coattails as God passed by. Even then, the only way Moses survived such a visitation was that God placed him in the cleft of the rock so that he would not completely go mad. (See Exodus 33:18-23.)

Ministers find themselves chasing those coattails. The pursuit is a lifelong journey, and we will never catch them. We are not supposed to. We must pause in the cleft of the rock and wait for the One who called us. This One can find us again and give us what we need and what we can have. The waiting takes faith.

It gets dry in the cleft. I hope that we will look carefully to those who are waiting with us in other clefts. Take some water. Offer it to the thirsty. We will need that same water ourselves.

The witches have it. We must be careful not to become too thirsty and too alone.

The ministry . . . Those of us in it know that if we are still in it, we are "still crazy after all these years."

Clergy Sexual Misconduct

In our United Methodist Conference report book, most items take up a few paragraphs. The report on ministerial sexual misconduct takes up five single-spaced pages. What is wrong with this picture?

A recent study has shown that 37 percent of ministers interviewed reported that they had engaged in sexual behavior inappropriate for a minister.[1] An analysis of this study concludes:

> Since the incidence of such behavior occurs three to four times more often among ministers than among other major helping professions [11 percent for psychologists], one can only conclude that ministry is hazardous in that the temptation to be sexually unfaithful is ever present and the resistance to this temptation is not as strong as the expectations of society or the historical standards of the profession require.[2]

The ministry requires a certain passion in order to do the work with enthusiasm and zeal. Alan Jones equates the love for ministry with the passion of a romantic affair.[3] Obviously, this same passion, when not properly channeled, can get ministers into a lot of trouble. Jones writes of this problematic acting out of our passions:

> I have known clergy who feel trapped in their bodies. Those struggling to be celibate and to play a black-suited role in the community often burst headlong out of their prison in the effort to connect with another human being. When I lived in New York, I would hear of ministers who would slip out of their uniforms and into their jeans and go cruising anonymously

in Greenwich Village looking for connections. For one brief damaging and inappropriate moment they would imagine themselves held and loved. It would then be time to return to the isolating prisonhouse of the ordained ministry. With help, many clergy have been able to make the journey back into their bodies and find ways to be intimate that are not destructive.

We need help sorting out the difference between our inner selves and our roles. People expect us to be mother, father, husband, wife, and lover. When our unacknowledged need connects with another's projection onto us, both of us pay heavily.[4]

The key words in the above quotation are "unacknowledged need." The minister's role covers up the minister's humanity like the robe conceals the clothes on Sunday morning. The humanity is still there. This covering becomes part of the problem.

Ministers know the feeling we get when someone says to us with a smile, "After all, ministers are human, too." We smile back and think while not saying, If you only knew how human.

The comment about our "human too" status is meant to give the minister a strange sense of absolution. We are to be somewhat human but not quite. We know that we are totally human with fig leaves and robes covering our own concealed reality.

It is this unacknowledged humanness that gets ministers in trouble. Whether clergy as a group are actually more sexually complex than other professionals is a mystery. We are expected not to be.

Urban Holmes points to the spotlight in which clergy find themselves:

American religion is obsessed with the "warm sins" such as illicit sex and gluttony . . . . What we fail to realize is that pastor or priest who succumbs to the sins of passion is fallen in the same manner as a fallen soldier. These are demons that threaten anyone who sets out upon the path through chaos. Some will lose.[5]

Ministers are the ones who supposedly know the demons' names. We are also the ones who should remember that the demons know our names. To fall victim to sexual passion is easy for the minister. We find ourselves in all kinds of places where the demons like to play and deceive. The one who stands near the fire can get burned. It is not as surprising as some would think.

When all the above are combined with the reality that sexuality and spirituality seem to share the same source of power, it is no wonder that clergy need warning labels tattooed to the insides of our souls. We both set ourselves up for the fall and often find ourselves set up.

There must be some way for clergy to constantly check ourselves out in this area. Obviously, for married clergy the need to care for the marriage is essential. The truth is that we get busy doing the Lord's work and forget that the same Lord is not happy when we sacrifice our families at the altar of work.

A good counselor will tell a couple that "your marriage comes before your children." It is just as wise a counsel for the minister to remember that the marriage relationship should be set before the vocation of ministry. If this is not done, the seeds of trouble will be planted. There will be many times that circumstances will shove the marriage into second place. Strong marriages can handle such occasional displacements; weak marriages will not. Far too many ministers have discovered this truth.

Single ministers with intimacy needs are subject not only to be set up by their congregations in loving yet manipulative ways, but are also set up for the demons calling to them. The fact that we are ministers does not change our animal nature. We are the highest order of God's creation, but we are of that order, not above it. Our instincts are strong. Instincts combined with the desire for being held and accepted is a volatile mix. Combine these needs with the unique vulnerabilities within ministry and the situation is dangerous.

Ask David. He was only human. In fact, that is why God picked the "runt of the litter." God must have known about David's nurturing of his passions on those lonely nights under the stars as he tended the sheep. David was a boy of great longings of which no one knew. His father, Jesse, almost forgot about the least of his sons when it came time to look for a candidate for king.

God needed a passionate leader for the unruly kingdom. God needed a person who was both a crafter of poetry and one who could be creatively deceptive in his leadership style. God needed someone foolish enough to not ask too many questions about just how big this Goliath was. But God also needed someone smart enough to structure a political network among diverse peoples.

God wanted passion. God got it. The trouble was that David forgot the truth that passion mixed with power can be very problematic. David's longings became sinful when he lost the need to be held accountable.

The same passions that led the young boy to be king also led him to Bathsheba's bed. These were not different passions. They were from the same source. There was not a good King David and a bad King David. It was the same man. When he lay with Bathsheba, he was still the passionate boy who was beloved of God. David simply forgot to test the spirits. The writer of poetry no longer felt understood by the nation he had created. He wanted to be understood and known by someone who would hold the "boy." Kings have unmet needs, and kings, like clergy, have a kind of power that can be dangerous.

David is a long-ago example of how those with power can rationalize what they do. This rationalization can become insulated, so that the person abusing the power no longer feels or sees the real effect of what he or she is doing.

Many clergy have fallen in love with another because they needed to fall in love. They had not found love in the hard places of their marriages, so they found it when life was broken open in front of them. Love became the absolver of action. It felt right.

It took Nathan to remind David. The biblical story is itself a reminder that reminders often come too late. David could have looked earlier into the mirror of his soul and discovered the image of the boy who needed to be held. He could have sensed the danger of his passions reflected next to the child who was beloved of God. It was the same image.

But David became blind because of the isolation of his power. Power needs constant correctives. Ministers need to understand this. We are privileged to stand in positions of sacred power. We are the ones there when life splits open. Oftentimes this splitting open is in very private spaces, in the privacy of home or office. We walk down paths that others are not allowed to walk. Those paths can lead to gardens of passion and desire where soft voices of serpents still whisper.

The minister, like the adolescent, needs to pay attention to feelings, passions, and longings before the moment in which these internal powers take control. How many parents have tried to convey to adolescents the reality that decisions about sexual behavior must be made before the time of passion in the backseat? It is too late then. Passions have a mind of their own. Paths, once taken, can lead us where we know we should not be.

Our biblical story tells us that our wills have, in fact, been altered. We are on the outside of the garden. To think that we are completely in control is the first whisper of the deceiver. David's control led him to feel that he could do what he wanted to do simply because he had the freedom to do it.

David's scheming to have Uriah killed reflects how entangled the web of passions can become. Excuses become reasons. Serpents' voices begin sounding like soft breezes in our souls. Someone needs to help us recognize voices for who and what they are. If our power keeps us too isolated, we will mistake the voices.

Ministers, like kings, need someone who can point the staff of judgment and discernment. It is obviously better if the staff can be pointed before it is too late.

For David it was too late. He lost a son. He lost part of his soul. He did not, however, lose his relationship to the God who still called him beloved. He also did not lose his ability to be king. His rule may have been compromised, but the God who anointed him king knew that David was still the passion-filled leader for the nation.

One of my greatest pains is to see how we ministers treat those of our own who fall victim to passions, especially the sexual ones. It is as if sexual misconduct is the unforgivable sin. Once the minister steps over this line, there is no going back.

Our ecclesiastical judicial systems usually act quickly in attempts to rid the body of the cancer. While we must not overlook sexual misconduct, it is apparent that an Old Testament process usually takes over. Are we not people of a new covenant who need to be aware that those who practice the mysteries of the faith are themselves wounded practitioners? Alan Jones states:

The Church is notoriously bad about handling the weaknesses and sins of its ordained ministers. One hears of congregations missing opportunities to confront, forgive, and
restore many a pastor. No one is to blame for this failure to
heal and to reconcile. We are all at fault. We all resist the
promise of the gospel. We are deaf to the Word. We also do
not know how to look after ourselves and to minister to one
another.[6]

I expect that the reason we have such trouble with the sins of
sexuality within the church is that most people within the
church are uncomfortable with the whole area of sexuality. In
the ministry, when one of us sins, we feel the damp cool of our
own shadow. For a moment, we recognize our own potential for
stepping over the line. We are both afraid and quick to judge.

A counselor once told me that adolescents have a difficult
time with fear but can more easily deal with anger. When I told
my sixteen-year-old daughter about her mother's recently diagnosed chronic illness, in hopes of getting emotional help from
my daughter, she reacted with anger. I needed her to be helpful
and understanding, but she became increasingly resentful and
angry. She could not handle her fear about her mother, so it came
out in anger.

Ministers seem to not do well with our fears about sexuality,
so we quickly judge others, often in an atmosphere of anger. The
people of our congregations do the same, especially when we
take the lead.

The way it is usually put is, "How could he have done
that?" It is a good question if it is asked slowly with the
emphasis on the "how." What circumstances led a minister
to act inappropriately?

Jesus is the one who made it possible to put the emphasis on
the "how" in such a question. The woman thrown at his feet
who was guilty of adultery was worthy of condemnation according to the Old Testament law. Jesus did not debate the law.
He took a deep breath and drew some doodles in the sand. He
so much as asked the question, How could she have done such
a thing? He asked the stone-carrying church crowd to ask the
same question. Was she "sinner number forty-six," or was she a

woman with a name and story? Was she "the woman caught in adultery," or was she a woman with a name and a "how"?

When one of the clergy commits a sexual indiscretion, is he or she simply another tainted white collar, or is there a story behind the collar and the sin? Judgment will be passed. The church is good at judgment, but is the One who called the church into being concerned with the judgment or the needed healing?

The church is scared to death of homosexuality. Why? Scripture can be cited that condemns the sin of homosexuality. I remind the church that this is exactly what the crowd did that day when Jesus had the adulterous woman at his feet. The crowd quoted Scripture. On the surface, the crowd was right. Jesus made the crowd go below the surface.

Why does the church seem to turn into an angry, fearful crowd when this subject is discussed? I think we are afraid before we are angry. I think the same Jesus knows this. Our reaction needs a Jesus who will ask us again to pause and listen. So often persons are quietly insecure about their own sexuality. We fear that which is different.

I do not want to start the debate again about homosexuality. I simply want the church to be the church and not the angry crowd. There will be an appropriate time for accountability. Clergy must always be held accountable for the way they act out their sexuality, but where is the grace we preach? Do we make an exception when it comes to breaches in sexual conduct? Is there not enough grace to go around for this area?

Ministers are sinners. We might as well all "come out of the closet" on that one. This coming out is not just about our sexuality; it is about our humanness. I do not know the source of sexual orientation. There are a lot of studies being done. The church needs to pause and listen, both to studies and to its Lord.

Healing in the area of sexuality is difficult because it reflects the deep and often not understood part of our beings. Ministers are called to be extremely careful when it comes to the way we act on our sexual longings and feelings. This care has its foundation in the unusual power we often hold.

We are to be held accountable. I just hope that the church will continue to ask the question, "*How* could he or she have done that?"

Clergy Burnout

The word *burnout* has been defined as "the emotional exhaustion resulting from the stress of interpersonal contact . . . in which helping professionals lose positive feelings, sympathy, and respect for their clients."[1] Much has been written lately about clergy burnout. It seems that the taboo has been revealed. A clergyperson is not exempt from the same stresses that other helping professionals encounter, even if he or she is "God's person." It has finally been exposed and documented that clergy do not receive some kind of inoculation against the perils of our life's work when the "hands are laid upon us." A Gallup poll reported that nearly one of every three ministers "had often or occasionally considered leaving the ministry because of the frustrations experienced in the role."[2]

Along with the stresses that other helping professionals experience, clergy experience some unique stresses of their own. Being God's person is a stress in itself. Ask Jeremiah.

Jeremiah is one of my favorite biblical characters because of the many ways he revealed his humanness. Though Jeremiah knew that he had been chosen by God, he did not hesitate to share his very human struggles with God.

Like many within the company of the ordained, Jeremiah at first resisted his call. His efforts at excuse making resembled a stammering Moses and a reluctant Jonah. But Jeremiah's bobbing and weaving did him no good. God did not give up. What God wanted, God got.

Jeremiah is a prime example of clergy burnout. The zeal of the Lord did consume him, as well as his own zeal. Jeremiah was a type-A hard worker. He did not know when to come up for air.

Clergy have often experienced that haunting sense of betrayal that comes when those they have been called to serve do not give back the needed affirmation and feedback. There is a great sense of sadness when love given is returned with an attitude that says, "You were paid to do it."

Jeremiah's way of sharing this exasperation goes like this:

Is evil a recompense for good?
　Yet they have dug a pit for my life.
Remember how I stood before thee
　to speak good for them,
　to turn away thy wrath from them.
　　　　　　　　　—Jeremiah 18:20

Jeremiah, like so many ordained types, had a high need to be accepted and liked. Even when he had to lay upon the people the harsh, judgmental Word of the Lord, Jeremiah hoped that his flock would still like him. This combination of the need to be stroked and the burden of the fire of the Lord's Word was tough for Jeremiah. It was a formula for burnout.

Jeremiah chronicles his path toward burnout:

O Lord, thou hast deceived me,
　and I was deceived;
thou art stronger than I,
　and thou hast prevailed. . . .
Cursed be the day
　on which I was born!
The day when my mother bore me,
　let it not be blessed! . . .
Why did I come forth from the womb
　to see toil and sorrow,
　and spend my days in shame?
　　　　　　　　　—Jeremiah 20:7,14,18

Jeremiah should be made the patron saint of all tired clergy who are feeling the loneliness that often comes with wearing the mantle of the Lord. Listen:

I did not sit in the company of merrymakers,
　nor did I rejoice;

I sat alone, because thy hand was upon me,
   for thou hadst filled me with indignation.
Why is my pain unceasing,
   my wound incurable,
   refusing to be healed?
Wilt thou be to me like a deceitful brook,
   like waters that fail?
                    —Jeremiah 15:17-18

Those last words that Jeremiah used to describe the God who had called him should ring in the soul of many of us who are ordained. The journey of ministry gets long and sometimes very dry. We are supposed to be the ones who lead our flocks to the green pastures beside the still waters. What happens when we feel like God has led us to a dried-up brook? What happens when we need some water to put out the slow-burning fire within us that is burning us out?

As mentioned previously, we often attempt to hide our dryness. We are afraid that no one will come to buy the waters we sell if we have dry throats. To even hint that God might not be coming through for us would be to reveal a family secret. Such hiding takes a tremendous amount of psychic energy and adds to the cycle of burnout.

Clergy need to know that we do not have to hide. One can get thirsty while trying to lead others to the waters. It happens. Remember Jeremiah.

Clergy need to know the warning signals and causes of burnout so that we will not end up somewhere along the journey with no water at all in our canteens. John Sanford, in his book *Ministry Burnout*, writes of nine special difficulties that lead to clergy burnout:

1. The job of the ministering person is never finished.
2. The ministering person cannot always tell if his [or her] work is having any results.
3. The work of the ministering person is repetitive.
4. The ministering person is dealing constantly with people's expectations.
5. The ministering person must work with the same people year in and year out.
6. Because he [or she] works with people in need, there is a

particularly great drain on the energy of the ministering person.

7. The ministering person deals with many people who come to her [or him] or the church not for solid spiritual food but for "strokes."

8. The ministering person must function a great deal of the time on his [or her] "persona."

9. The ministering person may become exhausted by failure.[3]

Add to this list the long hours, the parsonage situation for some, the demanding expectations of larger churches for growth and smaller ones for survival, and the strains of family concerns. The makings of the slow burn are gathered.

The expectations that clergy are supposed to keep it together and not get thirsty are themselves burdensome. Clergy need groups or individuals to help them check out the burnout level. Other people might not understand this, but clergy should. This is often why that person or the group may need to be other clergy.

Like Jeremiah, there are times when clergy find themselves dropped into "empty cisterns." Ministry takes us along paths where there are the empty, waiting pits. Sometimes we get dropped in, and sometimes we simply fall in.

Other clergy need to be constantly on the lookout for those of our number who are at the bottom of these dark places. As in Jeremiah 38:1-13, we may need to keep some rags around in order to lower them along with the lifesaving rope to our brothers and sisters and pull them out. These rags can be the remnants of our own woundedness, which we use to help others.

All clergy need pulling out at one time or another. We need to quit pretending that we do not need help. I have already mentioned the need for a "court fool" who would remind ministers of the need to do some good self-care. We need to lighten up because the burdens we carry are heavy. The fool needs to lift the bottoms of our robes and say with a smile, "Who is really under there?"

The answer to the question may frighten some. The one under the robe might be lonely and dry. That is okay. It does not feel good, but it comes with the turf. The burnout and the dryness do not mean that we are all used up or that we should get out or give up. It means we need water from someone who has a cup when our cup is out of reach. It means someone may need to listen in order to hear our slight cries from the bottom of empty cisterns.

Jeremiah discovered that he could not be the carrier of God's Word without experiencing tiredness. God had no trouble with Jeremiah's burnout. God knew it would be part of the task.

Dried-up brooks seem so barren to ministers because, hopefully, we know how the water tastes. Maybe this makes the dryness seem even more cruel. That is just the way it is.

The water *is* there or will be. Waiting is hard, especially when we are thirsty. We must be on the lookout for one another. We must keep our ears to the ground in order to hear the sounds of those who have fallen into dry cisterns.

Sanford closes his book with eight suggestions to help regain the energy lost in burnout. I share them now as rags to keep close by or cups of water for the journey:

1. Change your outer activity.
2. Develop creative relationships.
3. Use the body creatively.
4. Meditate.
5. Pay attention to dreams.
6. Keep a journal.
7. Pay attention to fantasies.
8. Use active imagination.[4]

The Wounds of Women in Ministry

I must begin this chapter with a confession. So far all of the biblical characters referred to in this inquiry about ministerial woundedness have been male. There are at least two reasons for this. First, it is because of my male-oriented paradigm and bias. It is that simple. I tend to see life and ministry from a male perspective to the detriment of being sensitive to a female perspective. The second factor is the bias of Scripture. It is somewhat of a miracle that there are any women held up as positive models in Scripture, considering the strong male orientation of the book we call holy.

Jesus had trouble getting the message across that new wine was not going to fit into the old wineskins. Jesus knew he was up against a prevailing "biblical" paradigm, which had as part of its foundation stories such as the one found in Judges 19. The terms *women* and *rights* did not belong together when viewed alongside such stories, which reveal the lack of rights of women in most of the biblical drama until the time of Jesus.

In the bizarre story recounted in Judges, a Levite sets out to retrieve his runaway concubine. He succeeds but finds himself in the house of an old man from the city of Gibeah. A crisis ensues when the house is surrounded by a group of "base fellows" who demand that the Levite be cast out of the house so that the men of the town can "know" him. Knowing what *to know* means in Old Testament language, one can picture the scene. As if this idea was not base enough, the old man responds,

"Do not act so wickedly; seeing that this man has come into my house, do not do this vile thing. Behold, here are my virgin daughter and his concubine; let me bring them out now. Ravish them and do with them what seems good to you; but against this man do not do so vile a thing." But the men would not listen to him. So the man seized his concubine, and put her out to them; and they knew her, and abused her all night until the morning (Judges 19:23-25).

It is not over. The Levite later takes a knife and divides up the poor concubine and ships her parts around the region to make a point. Biblical commentaries try to add some interpretation to this story of unbelievable cruelty toward women, but the effort fails to soften the reality that women were basically property.

This story needs Jesus. But before there is Jesus, there is the marvelous story of Esther. This book is in the Bible to shore up the observance of the Jewish Feast of Purim, but at least it portrays in a positive light the gifts of a woman who knew how to use power in a man's world.

Judy Rosener's work on the "feminine paradigm" points to the difference in leadership styles that women bring to a man's world. Her insights can help male clergy and female laypersons better understand the positive contributions that women bring to ministry.

Rosener delineates how feminine leadership is more interactive than male leadership. She goes on to show that female leadership tends to be encouraging and participatory, that it shares power and information, that it enhances other people's self-worth, and that it gets others excited about their work.[1]

Other research on the distinctiveness of women's leadership styles shows that women are more interested in establishing relationships than their male counterparts, who are more interested in power issues. Women work more toward consensus and are more accustomed to waiting, based upon their intuitive skills. Women are more apt to work from "experience" and allow more for "process." They are also more comfortable with issues surrounding vulnerability.[2]

The biblical story of Esther is a model of the feminine paradigm at work in a world hostile to its dynamics. Esther's story is paradigmatic for understanding the issues of women in ministry.

Esther, rather than simply blowing the whistle on the evil Haman, involved King Ahasuerus in the decision to cut Haman off at the knees. She could have done the male thing and simply made use of the power the king had given to her, but she let experience be a teacher. She brought together issues to allow learning to happen experientially instead of talking or lecturing about those issues.

The end result may seem to be the same. Haman got what was due him, and the Jewish people were saved from destruction. A closer look, however, reveals some of the uniqueness of the feminine paradigm at work. The king was allowed to see for himself the evils of the deceitful Haman. Esther set up a situation in which the king could "own" the decision of what to do with Haman, even though the king had earlier offered to Esther the opportunity to ask for anything she wanted.

Esther gathered the parties around the dinner table to allow full participation. She was patient in her efforts and set up a situation in which the CEO, in this case the king, ended up feeling excited about his decision. The king's decision was what Esther wanted all along.

The long-term results of such deliberate efforts by Esther were probably more enduring because of the way the king was allowed to own the decision. Esther knew what she was doing. She was thinking not only about community within the kingly, political court but also about the long-term effect the king's decision would have on the Jewish community's survival. Long before the term "team building" became popular, Esther understood its power.

In an environment in which 20 to 45 percent of seminary enrollment is female and the increase for women in seminary is 223 percent over the past ten years, the handwriting is on the wall.[3] Women will be in ministry even more in the future.

I cannot fully understand nor feel the wounds of the women who are in ministry. I see them from the distance of my male perspective, but I have observed some of these wounds. The resistance of a church dominated by male leadership can be documented.[4] Women in ministry often see the very gifts that come from their unique feminine paradigm misunderstood and used against them by the people they serve.

People are sometimes afraid of vulnerability, yet these same people need to face their vulnerability. Women inherently understand this issue better than men do. Women are often much better at communicating about sensitive issues; and yet, many times when women do this, they are perceived as weak rather than strong leaders.

Women fall victim to the same trap that male clergy get entangled in when they try to get others to do what some think the minister is "paid" to do. Women naturally try to involve people rather than doing work for them. People may resent this, but this is the New Testament way of doing things.

Studies have shown that when women pastors are given the chance to serve, the reaction to their leadership is mostly positive.[5] Women must be given the chance. A lot of pain for women in ministry comes at the point of not being given the chance.

If Mary, the mother of Jesus, had not been willing to struggle with certain vulnerability issues, we might not have a ministry called Christian. What if Mary had said no? Surely she had the choice. She was willing to say "let it be to me according to your word" rather than be intimidated or overly concerned about power issues.

Women can help men in ministry learn to take time, to take a chance, both of which women do naturally. In the present environment, men must assist women in order for them to have a chance to serve. After such assistance within the power structure, women have proven not only that they can lead but also that they add a new dimension to the ministry.

The sexual transference, which can be a problem with any minister, is more prevalent for women clergy since the issue of "sexuality" is automatically signaled because of the residue of a male-dominated culture and theology. Women have a harder time differentiating because of this transference by those they serve.[6]

I did not realize how much I can learn from women in ministry until I had the opportunity to work alongside women pastors. It is one thing to discuss women-in-ministry issues. It is quite another thing to learn by working with women in ministry.[7]

Ministerial Effectiveness

What does the phrase "ministerial effectiveness" really mean? What is the true measuring stick that should be used to determine what success is in ministry? Does "successful" mean the same thing as "effective"?

The only joy I gain from cutting my lawn is the sense of accomplishment I feel when I shut off the lawn mower and look at exactly what I have done. In my ministry, I cannot often see what I have accomplished. So much of what ministers do is hard to measure, but we do need some method of sensing accomplishment in ministry. Such lack of measurement of accomplishment has already been mentioned as one of the causal factors in ministerial burnout.

An old expression states, "If you do not know where you are going, you may end up some place else." Sometimes we ministers have no way of measuring where we are going. At other times we have no sense of ascertaining where we have been. Meanwhile, the judgment of our effectiveness is often done by the people we serve. The various barometers used by congregations are legion.

Being defined by the people we serve can feel good, but it is always dangerous. If we let others tell us who we are for too long, we begin to lose the self-differentiation that is needed for good psychological health.

Ministers who do not feel good about themselves can be as problematic as ministers who feel too good about themselves. One type is always trying to make up for something, while the other type is blind to the need for self-evaluation. Combine this reality with the unique power that ministers have and there is the potential for abuse and pain.

The ministry, as a profession, is hurting of late because of the awkwardness in our ability to measure effectiveness. There is much mediocrity within the ministry. Much of it is due to the standards that are not adhered to in evaluating effectiveness in ministry.

I heard one retired United Methodist bishop speak to this issue at a recent conference. This bishop stated that because of the mediocrity he had witnessed in ministry and the number of persons serving churches who should not be, he had changed his advice to local boards of ministry. In this bishop's earlier days, he advised boards who were in doubt about a certain candidate for ministry to pass the candidate and hope for improvement and maturation. Now this bishop's advice is "If there is any doubt, vote no."

This bishop had become aware through experience what earlier chapters in this book have documented: the ministry needs people who are not only called but who are psychologically healthy. The ministry attracts more than its share of persons who are struggling with certain emotional needs. This reality needs to be embraced by those committees and boards of review who are evaluating candidates for ministry.

Willingness and call are not enough. If we take the ministry seriously, then we need to take the time and effort to make sure that candidates for ministry are relatively healthy in their psychological makeup before they receive the blessing of the church to go on for ordination.

What, then, is the measure for effectiveness of those who are in ministry? Simon Peter is a good model to use in viewing this issue.

Peter was eager and full of zeal. He was certain of his call and had no trouble taking a leadership role. He had given up much to follow Jesus and was certain of his own commitment—certain until he broke under pressure. If we hold Peter up as a role model for ministerial effectiveness, he will give us a clue to the problem.

Peter's efforts to walk on water are a prime example of the issues that need to be dealt with when it comes to effectiveness in ministry. Peter thought that he knew the technique needed to follow Jesus out there on the water. He wanted to "walk where Jesus walked." To be able to say that he had done the water-walking thing would give him ultimate credibility as a religious leader. So why was Peter not judged to be effective in his faith walk? He had failed to ask some important questions first. The first question should not have been "Can I walk on this water like Jesus?" The first question should have been "Do I believe in and trust in this man enough to walk and not look down?"

This question was not answered until after the resurrection, when Jesus fixed breakfast for Peter and gave the wounded disciple a chance to answer the question "Do you really love me enough?" Peter had thought of himself as effective when he led the delegation that last evening around the dinner table. "I'll never desert you, Lord . . . not me . . . no failure here." What Peter failed to realize was that he was again using the wrong criteria for measurement. He used it around the table, and he used it around the boat at the water-walking episode.

Peter wanted results without having first spent some very special time with his Lord, time that needed to be spent dealing with some critical and primary issues. These issues were to be the foundation for judging later effectiveness. These were issues of honesty and issues revolving around just how much Peter was willing to pay and suffer in order to be a true follower.

Sitting around scrambled eggs and fish and still surrounded by failure and reality, Peter was given the chance to judge his effectiveness. Having faced what pain and failure he was willing to endure, Peter had come up with some more stable measurements for effectiveness. Peter had learned that, while he thought success meant walking on water, it might be more effective to stay in the boat and spend some more time with Jesus around certain key issues.

Norman Shawchuck and Roger Heuser offer a guide to examining ministerial effectiveness. They write that the secret of effective leadership in ministry can best be seen by examining four crucial steps:

1. How to keep your heart for God alone, and the passion of your call burning in your belly;
2. How to keep yourself out of the activity trap;

3. How to continue lifelong learning;
4. How to influence all persons who serve in paid or volunteer positions to perform.[1]

These writers go on to describe how one can begin to evaluate ministerial effectiveness through the use of a four-quadrant model. The four quadrants are: I–urgent important matters, II–not urgent important matters, III–urgent unimportant matters, and IV–not urgent unimportant matters. Quadrant I consists of such items as crises, deadlines, problems, and serious misunderstandings among lay leaders. Quadrant II consists of building relationships among pastoral staff and lay leaders, planning time off for reflection, continuing education, and sabbath. Quadrant III consists of some telephone calls, mail, reports, meetings, and interruptions. Quadrant IV is made up of busy work, trivia work, some telephone calls, reports, meetings, and time wasters.

Shawchuck and Heuser conclude that "the heart of managing [ministerial] effectiveness is in Quadrant II." By dealing with matters that are not urgent but important, the matters in Quadrant I are slowly reduced, and the matters in the other quadrants take on the needed perspective.[2]

Peter discovered what relational consultants have always known: We do not learn from experience; we learn from reflecting on our experience. Peter wanted to get on with ministry. What he needed to do was examine *why* he wanted to do ministry. He also needed some time for self-inventory and a good way to do some faith analysis. He discovered that he had some work to do before he jumped out onto or into the water.

Ministers get so caught up in the work of ministry that they get lost in the busy nature of the work. They are like the airline pilot who announced to his passengers the good news and the bad news: "The bad news, ladies and gentlemen, is that we are lost; I have no idea where we are. The good news is that we are making excellent time."

Some pastors have found that even though the congregation's evaluation of their ministry seems to be one of "making excellent time," they are in fact lost—not sure of where they have been or where they are going. Alongside this reality are the expectations of the judicatory for effectiveness or success.

Outside measurements should always be held up to the light for analysis. As Eugene Peterson bluntly puts it: "A successful pastor will discover a workable program and repeat it in congregation after congregation to the immense satisfaction of [his or] her parishioners. The church members can be religious without praying or dealing with God. Prostitute Pastor."[3]

One of Peterson's major themes in most of his writings is the urging of pastors not to buy into the modern view of what an effective pastor is. He writes:

> The people in our congregations are, in fact, out shopping for idols. They enter our churches with the same mind-set in which they go to the shopping mall, to get something that will please them or satisfy an appetite or need. John Calvin saw the human heart as a relentlessly efficient factory for producing idols. Congregations commonly see the pastor as the quality-control engineer in the factory. The moment we accept the position, though, we defect from our vocation. . . . Living in golden calf country as we do, it is both easy and attractive to become a successful pastor like Aaron.[4]

In the work I have done with wounded pastors, many of them have not spent enough time in Quadrant II. Many have bought into trying to be the quality-control engineer for the religious warehouse. Like Peter, we want to walk on water. We want to do ministry without first reflecting on the "why." We need to first have breakfast with Jesus.

In times of reflection and centering, we might discover that we are trying to be successful while losing effectiveness. Other pastors get completely lost in the swamp of mediocrity and are neither successful nor effective. The church gets too comfortable with this swamp. The institutional church has lived so long near the swamp that they think it is the only lake around.

Maloney and Hunt offer another helpful guide to viewing ministerial effectiveness. They suggest that true effectiveness is not always judged from just looking at the bottom-line numbers and statistics. Effectiveness in ministry should not be based simply on what seems successful. Effectiveness should be "evaluated in terms of whether [ministers] have been influential in reconciling people to God through the ministrations of the church."[5]

These researchers conclude that ministerial effectiveness must take into account the primary criteria of changed insights, changed understandings, and changed attitudes.[6] In other words, it is vitally important to view the measurement of how influential a minister has been on the spiritual maturation process of those he or she is serving. Statistics can be used simply to baptize success, while, in fact, statistics might be low and effectiveness of ministry might be high.

Peter's track record looked good. He was enthusiastic. He had a well-worked-out plan for what was going to be a great church-growth model. Workshops were planned on "water walking," and there were going to be large rallies held to show people how to say with grand enthusiasm, "You are the Christ, the son of the living God." What Peter had not learned was that the long road to be taken for ministerial effectiveness involved a lot of time spent examining the insights and attitudes behind why he wanted his church to do all these things. It took his own spiritual maturation process, which was laced with pain and failure, to show Peter the need to deal with items that were important but did not seem urgent.

We ministers will constantly be told what it is that makes us effective. Whether it be the number of hospital visits made or souls added to the rolls, someone or some agency will hold up a measuring stick. Many of the statistics and programs established are part of what effectiveness might mean, but behind the doing is the critical need for reflection as to why we do what we do. We need to spend time with the One who called us. That call is to first be a follower before we do anything, including walking on water.

Part II

Using the Enneagram to Understand Ministerial Leadership Styles

The Enneagram Charts

The following charts reflect general knowledge about the Enneagram. The various names or titles assigned to the different Enneagram numbers vary according to the author or instructor.

Diagrams 1, 2, and 3 reflect general Enneagram theory. More knowledge about these names and numbers can be obtained by reading some of the books listed in the bibliography at the end of this section.

The diagram entitled "Enneagram Ministerial Types" is my own creation. It is offered as a tool to assist ministers in applying Enneagram theory to various ministerial leadership styles.

Diagram #1

The Enneagram

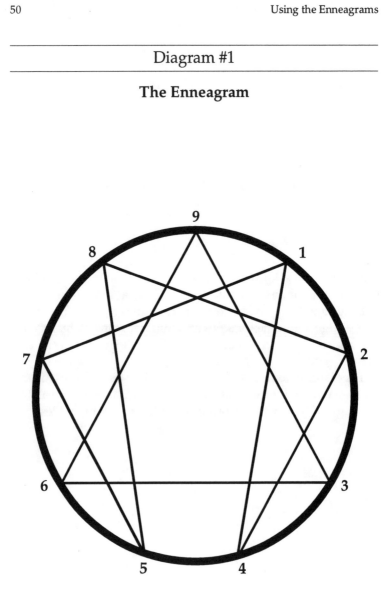

Diagram #2

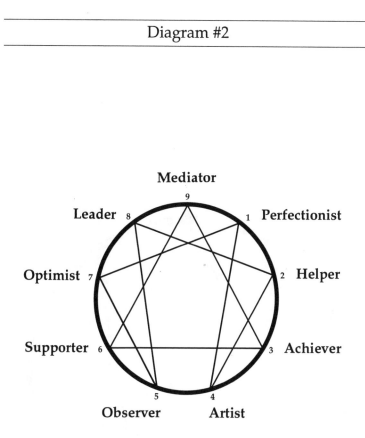

Eilis Bergin and Eddie Fitzgerald, *An Enneagram Guide: A Spirituality of Love in Brokenness* (Mystic, Conn.: Twenty-Third Publications, 1993), 14. Used by permission.

Diagram #3

The Compulsive Types

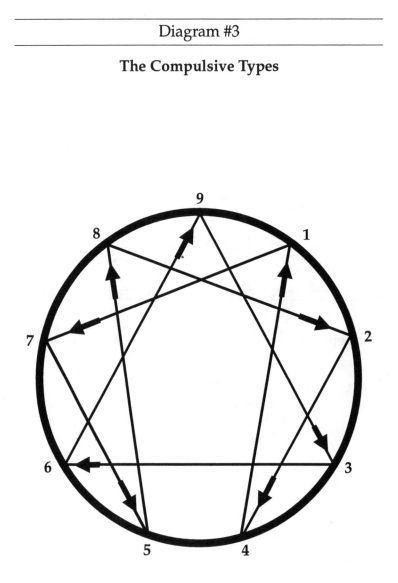

The Direction of Growth and Development

Diagram #4

Enneagram Ministerial Types

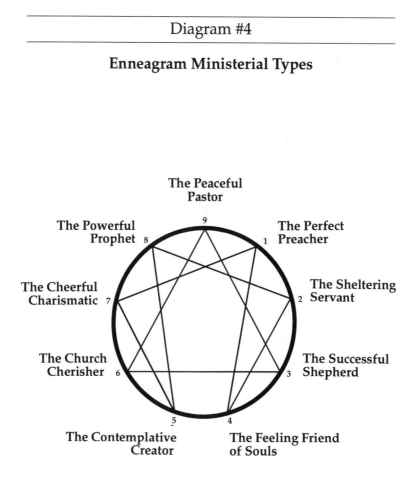

The Peaceful
Pastor

The Powerful
Prophet 8

The Perfect
Preacher 1

The Cheerful
Charismatic 7

The Sheltering
2 Servant

The Church
Cherisher 6

The Successful
3 Shepherd

The Contemplative
Creator

5

The Feeling Friend
4 of Souls

Explanation of the Enneagram

The most helpful tool I have ever encountered to understand myself and others is the Enneagram. This ancient tool for self-understanding is a wonderful asset in the area of spiritual direction.

Much has been written about the Enneagram. It is not my purpose in this brief section to completely explain the Enneagram or its implications for spiritual formation. What I do offer is a brief overview of this tool for self-understanding. I will then transpose the interpretive categories of the Enneagram onto various ministerial leadership styles.

It is my belief that all ministers need a way to better understand how personality affects ministry. The Enneagram offers a way for a person to move toward a direction of integration in order to gain both self-understanding and fulfillment. Fundamental to my reason for writing this book is the belief that we who are ministers need a better grasp of our own personalities. Within these personality structures are the specific needs that drew us to ministry. Surrounding these needs are our unique strengths and weaknesses.

The Enneagram can be a very user-friendly methodology to understand who we are and where we came from. It is also a much-needed resource for the minister in the area of helping others in their spiritual journeys.

The Enneagram can help the minister face the needs and defenses of the ego. This search is critical. John Sanford points out why:

> It takes a great deal of energy to maintain our egocentricity. Only the creative life brings us vital energy for living; the egocentric life drains energy from us. As the years go on it becomes harder and harder to maintain our egocentric posture successfully, as its satisfactions and reassurances are only temporary, and sooner or later we will burn out.
>
> Fortunately, our Christian tradition helps us. Jesus once said, "Whoever will come after me, let him deny himself, and

take up his cross, and follow me" (Mark 8:34, KJV). From the viewpoint of religious psychology, to take up one's own cross means to take up the task of becoming a whole person. The cross is a place of death and eventual rebirth. What must die is the ego-centric Ego. What rises is the new Ego, related to the Creative Self. This is why C. G. Jung once remarked that the emergence of the Self is always the defeat of the Ego. What is defeated is our egocentricity, and though we may fear and shun the psychological life crisis that will bring this about, there is nonetheless salvation within it. This theme is like a thread running through all of Christianity, the theme expressed by Jesus when He said that he who loses his life will find it. So the loss of the egocentric life is the discovery of the genuine Self, and the Christian images point the way through.[1]

I have discovered in my life, my ministry, and in working with the wounds of other ministers that not facing the needs of the ego leads to a lot of games and a lot of pain. Ministers hide not only behind robes but behind their egos. Most often this is not a conscious hiding. The Enneagram makes this hiding apparent. Healing can take place when we face our true selves.

At the end of this section are listed a number of books that can be utilized to gain an in-depth understanding of the Enneagram. This overview is simply a "Reader's Digest" attempt at explanation to whet your appetite.

I have used the Enneagram often in my own local church, with individuals and groups, and with ministerial renewal retreats. I have never used anything that had more of an impact on people than this ancient tool for spiritual direction.

The word "Enneagram" simply means "the nine points." Its origin is veiled in mystery, but it is generally accepted that the Sufis used it as a way of explaining the difference in peoples' religious understanding. The Sufis (a mystical movement within Islam) called the Enneagram "the face of God."

The Enneagram became somewhat popular because of its use by the Jesuits in their efforts at spiritual formation and spiritual direction. Many books have been published in the last few years seeking to interpret the Enneagram. Various type indicators are now available to be used by individuals. These inventories, or tests, help a person ascertain which of the nine numbers he or she is.

The theory of the Enneagram basically states that, as children, we all learned a basic pattern of survival. This survival pattern was based on genetics and reinforced by our actions as we were parented. To put it simply, we learned what worked, and we became compulsive around a certain pattern of behaviors and feelings.

This compulsion soon began to be the way we perceived all of life. We did not realize that this compulsive way of viewing life blocked out eight other views of life. We learned to pay attention to life in one certain way to the exclusion of other ways. This style of attention became our ego or personality.

The theory of the Enneagram goes on to state that the first part of our life is spent fortifying this ego structure or personality. It is what worked for us, but remember that the word *personality* is derived from the Greek word *persona* which means "mask."

In the second half or "task" of life, a certain restlessness develops because it is time to unlock the personality and take a look at its compulsions and time to take off the mask. This unlocking or stripping-away process becomes the necessary "second task" of life. The defensive ego may fight it, but it is the pathway that leads to ongoing spiritual growth. This unlocking is usually resisted by the ego because it feels like death, but remember what Jesus said about dying to the self.

In order to really look at ourselves, the Enneagram theory refers to something called a "fair witness" or an ego observer. This observer stance is needed in order to adequately see the compulsions that we tend to live by. In order to see what before has been hidden, there needs to be some tearing away of the ego. Spiritual growth is painful.

The cycle Jesus offered is one of death and resurrection. In order for new life to happen, there usually needs to be some form of death to the old. The Enneagram gives a pathway for this death to happen so that new life can emerge.

When I did my own Enneagram work, it was scary. It was as if someone, for the first time in my life, opened the door of my soul and walked around inside. When I was helped to establish "the observer," there was outlined a description of me that only my secret self knew. Before me were explanations of things that I had hidden. There was light shed on dark places of which only I had knowledge.

I was cracked open. I saw my "shadow." My giftedness and my sin were both exposed. It was painful, but so is birth—and death. I understood things about myself that I had walked by all of my life. Most importantly for this effort in understanding the wounds of ministry, I saw in the open light for the first time why I entered the ministry and why I was the kind of minister I was, warts and all.

The Enneagram also offered me a clear path for growth and some distinct warning signals of how my kind of personality can get in trouble. Using the Enneagram in combination with the Christian story and tradition can be a powerful tool for spiritual direction and self-understanding.

What I propose to do is give a brief description of the nine compulsive types and show how these types are reflected in various ministerial leadership styles. I offer this not just as a way of labeling people but as a way to find the place from which a person starts a journey.

When we deny that we are compulsive in the way we see and live life, then we are trapped and do not even know it. We say things like "That's just the way I am." There is freedom on the other side of such fatalistic statements. We must face the psychological truth that the way we see life is not the way life really is.

Much of the pain in ministry comes from our blindness. If we can ever see that "the emperor is indeed naked" and that we are the emperor, then we can shed the needed tears that precede redemption and laugh the joyous laugh of freedom, which comes with salvation and healing.

The Nine Enneagram Types

The naming of the nine types varies, depending upon which interpreter of the Enneagram one chooses to read. Richard Rohr's typology will be used as part of my description of the Enneagram. Rohr describes the nine types in caricature fashion, since one way of breaking open the ego and its compulsions is to hold it up in exaggerated form. He also portrays the nine compulsive types in terms of the "need to be" something.[1]

The names given to ministerial leadership styles are my own doing. These names are also meant to be an exaggeration in order to highlight the compulsive view of each number.

Type One: The Need to Be Perfect (The Perfectionist)

The Perfect Preacher

This person learned as a child that he or she was okay if everything was in order and made right. A Type One becomes angry when things are not right. This compulsive type has little patience with those who do not "get with the program" and make things orderly and functional.

The anger of a One is kept within and may come out as self-righteousness. Ones are hard workers and cannot understand people who are not. They tend to be very hard on themselves and often have strong negative voices within them that come from childhood. These voices tell them over and over again, "You are good if you work hard and make things right."

This is the "perfect preacher" kind of minister. The desk is neat. The sermon is structured. The committees of the church are or should be in order. The One minister may also suffer from indigestion, stress-related illnesses, and other symptoms that come from not releasing anger.

The One's calling to ministry may have been wrapped around the need to get things right in life. He or she may feel a lot of pressure to straighten things out.

Ministry can be frustrating for Ones because churches tend to be messy places, both emotionally and sometimes organizationally. If Ones can exercise control in a church, things tend to run smoothly. This control need can cause real trouble, however, when the preacher cannot keep control close in hand or if too many others want control of the church.

In the Enneagram, the direction for growth and integration for a One is toward the Seven, the Cheerful Charismatic, because there is the need for the One to lighten up. The One must get in touch with his or her feelings and not simply rely on actions. Type One ministers must learn that growth is not a static thing and will necessarily involve risk, mystery, feelings, and mess-ups. These ministers need to find time for play. They need to not be so hard on family, themselves, or congregations. Ones need to be able to smile and realize that there is really no such thing as a perfect preacher.

Type Two: The Need to Be Loved and to Love (The Helper)

The Sheltering Servant

The Two, in Enneagram theory, is the person whose identity is measured by the many ways in which he or she tries to help people. These people love to care about others. What they often do not realize is that their need to care for others stems from their need for others to care for them.

There are a lot of Twos in the ministry, and there is a lot of Two in most ministers. This is not surprising since other research mentioned in this book has pointed to the needy nature of most ministers. As mentioned earlier, there is nothing wrong with this reality *if* we become more aware of it. Underlying causes for our need to help others must be brought out into the light so that we will not project certain personal needs onto those we serve.

Ministers will be healthier persons if we quit pretending that we help others only because we are "servants of God." Hopefully we *are* servants, but we are also persons who have the need to help others. This need is often deeper than is fully recognized and can be the cause of emotional pain.

What is important about the way the Enneagram works is that it helps ministers embrace our own compulsions and see them for what they are. If we do this, we can become more free and will not be so used by our internal compulsions. We can acknowledge the mixed motives behind many of our actions,

confess our sometimes inordinate needs, and go on to do our
work in the freedom of God's grace, remembering that we serve
a God who uses broken people and mixed motives.

Twos love to be loved. They can be manipulative and will
turn on people who do not return their love in the proper
manner. Twos like to be affirmed for their caring and internally
are prideful about their level of commitment and caring.

The ministerial type that fits the Two personality I call the
Sheltering Servant. The suffering servant image has been held
up before ministers as an ideal for ministerial leadership. This
is fine, except there sometimes needs to be an examination of
why we suffer.

Some ministers care in extreme ways because they are trying
to prove something. They are trying to prove how acceptable
they are, to prove that people need to love them and appreciate
them.

I have a minister friend who is a Two. He would visit the
hospital to care for a sick parishioner when he was sick himself.
He has left his family at times when they needed him because
he had to go and care. He has stayed at the church "too long" in
order to do a good job of caring. Recently he went into a deep
depression because he had not taken the time to care for himself.

Twos must stop and look at their motives for caring. They
must realize that there is a lot of self in their need to be sheltering
servants. Two ministers must work at a proper understanding
of self-love that is not dependent on what others think of them.

The path of growth for the Two minister is in the direction of
the Four, the Feeling Friend of Souls. This is because Twos must
get in touch with their real feelings. Fours tend to be too self-reflective, while Twos are not self-reflective enough. Fours think
too much about their specialness, while Twos do not think they
are special unless they are being noticed by people for how they
care.

Twos need to embrace their ulterior motives for caring and
become free to really care for others and themselves without
having to prove something. God knows our motives. We are not
kidding God, even if we are fooling ourselves and others. God
still cares for "servants" even if the motives are not pure.

A good test for a Two is to do something for someone else but make sure that no one else knows about it. This may be internally painful for a Two, but the pain can lead to growth.

Twos are needed, but they will be even better care-givers and more proportionate in their caring if they will be honest and reflective about their motives. These sheltering servants need the shelter of the divine caring of God to expose their ego needs so they can truly be free to care.

Type Three: The Need to Succeed (The Achiever)

The Successful Shepherd

The Type Three minister will usually dress for success. The robe will be just right. He or she knows the role of the minister and plays it to the max. Three ministers are good at what they do. They work long hours and want to be the best in terms of performance.

The term "successful shepherd" brings together the problem for the Three minister. Tension is created between professionalism and the call to be a self-giving shepherd. The shepherd often has to give up something for the "success" of the sheep. The task for the Three minister is to not lose the shepherd's heart in the midst of striving to be successful.

As children, Threes learned that to be okay they had to perform and do well. The problem is that they did this to the detriment of their internal feelings. Threes are so concerned with image that they have not spent enough time with feelings.

The Three minister wants to look good, not just be good. The successful shepherd knows how to convince the sheep that he or she is what they need in a leader. Bishops and judicatory leaders are often Threes. They know what it takes to appeal to a group.

This image and appeal are not inherently bad. What is called for is an awareness by a Three that some internal work needs to be done and not just external. For Threes to become whole, they need to move toward the Six, the Church Cherisher. The Six perspective will help them be honest about their motives and help them see reality from the group perspective and not just an individual perspective.

Since Threes are so concerned with image, it is a temptation for them to become entangled in deceit and lies in order to protect the image they have created. I have observed that many of the wounds in ministry happen because of an effort to keep up this Three image and energy.

Failure is terrifying for a Three minister. Shepherds, however, must risk failure in order to be true keepers and leaders of the sheep. The gospel offers the leader the opportunity to fail in order to gain. The Christian minister must struggle with what success means in light of a leadership style that has as its focus a cross.

The Three energy is also central to the competition that is so prevalent in the ministry. Movement toward the Six perspective refocuses this competitive drive toward a cooperation motif centered around the needs of the group or body.

The institutional church thrives off of Three energy, but like the individual Three minister, the church also needs constant redemption. The body of Christ must always be asking, "What is below the image of what we are doing?"

Type Four: The Need to Be Unique or Special (The Artist)

The Feeling Friend of Souls

I am a Four who is a minister and have found great truth in this theory as a way to understand why I am the way I am. Fours usually had childhoods in which they developed some sense of loss. This could have been a real loss or a perceived loss. Fours, therefore, developed a deep sense of longing. They tend to be melancholy and creative.

Fours long to be seen as special by people, so their natural introversion is counteracted by the need to create in front of others who will then see their uniqueness. Fours have nurtured an active imagination and often live on the edge of many fantasies.

Four ministers have a hard time living in the present since they tend to either long for the past or fantasize about a hoped-for future. They are easily hurt by members of a congregation and tend to take things personally.

I have named the Four minister the Feeling Friend of Souls because of this type's high capacity for empathy. Fours literally feel with people. They often sense what is going on with individuals in their congregations. Fours are usually highly expressive, using images to convey the feelings of the people to whom they minister.

Unlike Three ministers, Fours stay too much in their inner world. They feel everything over and over. Fours have to learn to externalize certain feelings. This is the reason that the Four's movement toward integration is in the direction of the One. The Four minister needs to objectify feelings.

Fours cannot wait to feel that something is right for them. They must act sometimes before they feel or in spite of certain feelings. For a Four, feelings are reality. This can be wonderful and dangerous.

Fours have a natural tendency toward envy. I used to kick myself around emotionally when I heard one of my peers preach a good sermon only to discover myself feeling sudden envy. The first thing that came to my mind was "I wish I were up there doing that." This feeling used to make me feel ashamed (a typical feeling for Fours), but now I realize that this is simply my Four-ness showing its colors.

In Enneagram theory, there is a wonderful expression: "observe and let go." I have learned that when these feelings of envy come up, I must smile a bit at the silliness of my feelings and let them go. There is no point in holding on to the feelings, but they must be acknowledged for what they are. Claim it, name it, and tame it. These are words that fit well into Enneagram theory.

The Enneagram teaches that sin means "too much of a good thing is a bad thing." This is why the word "compulsion" is used to describe the various types. The way a person looks at life has its good qualities, but when this view becomes the only view, necessary reality is blocked and a blindness sets in.

Using myself as an example, if I am not aware of my need to be special, I will spend my energy trying to get something from people for myself. I will be controlled by my compulsion rather than managing it.

Fours tend to be very creative and artistic. (What would you expect me to say!) They can be excellent preachers and creators of liturgy or music. Their deep sense of the dramatic side of life allows them to uncover many feelings that are present in the gospel narrative.

Four ministers have to learn to live in the present and not dream about the next church to be served. They have to let go of past hurts, especially if someone has wronged them. Since Fours tend to personalize everything, they often need a spiritual director or support group who can get them to step out of themselves and see things more objectively.

Type Five: The Need to Perceive (The Observer)

The Contemplative Creator

If all ministers could be monks, Fives would be in heaven. Fives are very introverted people. They want to perceive rather than participate. They have a hard time sharing themselves and do not like to take risks, especially emotional ones.

For a Five to be called of God into parish ministry is really a dilemma. To be in parish ministry is hard for Fives because they are constantly called upon to be with people rather than observing them. Fives make excellent teachers. They can also organize detailed programs for others to do, but relational endeavors are hard for them.

Type Five ministers are good counselors because counseling can be seen as an exercise in perception. Since Fives can see things objectively without getting involved, they provide the needed atmosphere for good counseling.

Fives have a hard time being "at home" or being everybody's friend. They are often mistakenly viewed as being unfriendly, aloof, or uncaring. None of these labels are necessarily true for the healthy Five. The term "contemplative creator" best fits the Five minister. What is often seen as distant about them is really their posture of contemplation while they are putting something together in their inner selves.

Five ministers need to move toward the Eight, the Powerful Prophet. This will push them to get out of themselves and interact with life and people rather than just perceiving. Five ministers have to learn that feelings are also the source of insight and that they can learn by sharing themselves. The challenge of the Five is to offer more of themselves to the people they serve.

Five ministers have to constantly face the issue of commitment to others. They often fear commitment and must risk the needed involvement with others in order to grow as persons.

The Contemplative Creator has much to share from his or her own rich inner world. The church can be a better place if Fives will risk sharing their insights. The Five minister will, in turn, be a more whole person, having shared more of his or her inside world.

Type Six: The Need for Security (The Supporter)

The Church Cherisher

The ministry has a lot of Type Six people within its ranks. The reason is that the Type Six energy centers around the need to have an authority figure and a group to maintain that authority. Type Six ministers gain their identity by providing for the group's needs. Sixes learned as children that they were acceptable if they felt secure in a group. These people know how to please the group. They have a real ability to discover what it is that a group or an authority figure needs.

The Six minister fears insecurity and looks to law or guidelines in order to alleviate this insecurity. Six ministers tend to be judgmental of anyone who does not abide by the group norms. They often project any flaw within their own character onto the total group or an individual within the group. For this reason, Six ministers may end up moving from church to church because of such reasons as "The church did not support me" or "Those people simply would not let me be their pastor."

Sixes are sought out by organizations for obvious reasons. Institutions need people to lead the organization who will maintain the norms and champion its ideals. It is better for the institutional maintenance if the authority of the institution is not questioned. Sixes do institutional maintenance very well. That is the reason I have also labeled them the Body of Christ Booster.

Church growth principles are built around Six energy. Security, for the leader, is found as the group expands and becomes more cohesive around established group ideals. Type Six energy and leadership is needed in order for the institutional church to be a strong organization. The danger of the Six perspective is also the danger for the organized church.

Maintenance needs can obscure the needs of certain individuals within the church. Oftentimes fear is covered up by organizational needs. The major problem for Type Six ministers is fear. Somehow, as children, Sixes decided that the best way to overcome internal fear was to look to authority figures or organizations.

Fears need to be faced and not covered up by rules or organizational needs. The rise of fundamentalism is an example of extreme Six energy at work. The fear that the Bible and basic moral values are being eroded has led to the need for a kind of church that requires a visible authority figure. A Six church will be built around strict adherence to order and regulation.

The church needs Six ministers who have gained a sense of self-reflection. The healthy Six minister learns that integration comes from moving toward the Nine style of living, the Peaceful Pastor. In this movement, the Six realizes that, though the group is important, the individual must examine his or her own motives and agendas. This minister needs to face fears with a more open attitude and not project them onto the group. The anxiety that is very present to the Six is honestly seen, and a more relaxed style of attention is evident when the Nine corrective is introduced.

Historically, the body of Christ has needed to question its Six way of seeing life. If this does not happen, the church becomes too rigid and exclusive in its scope. The health of the church needs Six leadership, but this leadership must be open to individuals who will at times question certain guidelines and methods of maintenance.

The anxiety that is often felt in churches may be the result of an unquestioned Six energy. Religion, at its best, is not a covering up of fear but a facing of fear in the light of the hope offered through faith. The Six minister must always struggle to balance the group's needs and individual perspectives that might challenge the group's authority.

It is my opinion that one reason we ministers have not been more open to a closer examination of the woundedness within our ranks is because of the prevalence of the Six energy. We need the group to be strong and look healthy. Ministers often project their own shadows onto other wounded clergy in order to protect the self and the primary group. Fear underlies this projection.

It is easy to hide in the group. We need to face our own insecurities apart from the needs of the group. The group, if it is healthy, can then help the individual grow as his or her fears are faced.

One reason that wounded ministers are so quickly cast out of the church is because of an overbearing and sometimes unhealthy Six energy that fears any flaw in the body. Purity is often mentioned as the motive for such casting out, but fear is behind many such actions.

Accountability needs to be maintained in order for standards to be upheld and credibility to be continued, but the gospel has within its very core the reality of the fallenness of all persons. This fallenness includes ministers who hide behind robes and rules. The Enneagram is one way to begin to help us come out of our hiding places.

Type Seven: The Need to Avoid Pain (The Optimist)

The Cheerful Charismatic

I use the term *charismatic* in the description of the Type Seven minister not in its narrow sense but in its broader meaning. This broader understanding would include the idea of the enthusiastic sharing of good things of the Spirit. The Seven minister is interested in stimulation, both sensual and visual. This type of minister is full of enthusiasm and is always wanting things to happen.

The Cheerful Charismatic does not like to dwell on problems. He or she tends to be optimistic to a flaw. The reason behind this optimism is a fear of any kind of pain. Sevens learned as children that pain was wrong.

Sevens fill their lives with many different kinds of stimulation in order to avoid or cover over pain. Seven ministers usually have trouble with the concept of the cross, since it seems to focus on the pain of humanity. Sevens like Easter, joy, celebration, and lively ritual.

The church needs Seven leadership to help create life within places where enthusiasm is not the order of the day. Sevens tend to be very extroverted and gain part of their identity from being in the midst of people.

They usually love being the center of attention and often make excellent pulpiteers. Sevens are, for the most part, very engaging and entertaining people.

Seven ministers have to be careful in the area of depth. This is because they can be superficial if they do not nurture a quality of self-reflection about life. They care little for boring people and like life to be full of interesting events. They tend to spread themselves too thin and not take the time to get to the heart of certain matters, especially if it involves painful issues.

Sevens are always wanting to go on to the next thing. Activity is stimulating to them. Seven ministers pastor churches where a lot of things are happening.

The move toward growth for the Type Seven minister is in the direction of the Five, the Contemplative Creator. This movement helps them gain a certain reflective quality about their activity. It also helps them gain some depth about what their activity might mean. The Five energy enables Sevens to learn to be alone with themselves.

Inevitable pain needs to be faced by Sevens. This will help them better minister to the deep needs that accompany other people's pain. Optimism is needed in ministry, but not at the expense of refusing to face the darkness in life.

The smile of the Seven must be combined with the willingness to "weep with those who weep." When the Seven's charismatic, gift-filled enthusiasm is balanced with sensitivity to the suffering of others, wonderful ministry happens.

Type Eight: The Need to Assert Oneself (The Leader)

The Powerful Prophet

Ministers who are Eights come across as strong and powerful people. They learned in childhood to avoid vulnerability and to assert themselves in order to gain their identity. Eights are often perceived by others as being angry people. Oftentimes this is not anger but strength and assertiveness. Sometimes it is anger.

Type Eight ministers are good at pushing programs through and cutting to the essentials of a matter. They tend to command respect and do well in communities that need authority figures who are strong leaders.

Patience is not a primary quality of Eights, and they have little of it with those people who are whiny or weak. Eights do, however, have a true concern for the real underdogs of life. They are champions of causes and tend to be true prophets for social justice. Taking chances comes naturally for the assertive Eight.

I once saw what I believe to be a Type Eight minister emotionally undress another minister in front of an audience. The minister in the audience to whom this Eight was speaking made the mistake of implying that the speaker did not know what he was talking about. The Eight began asking the questioner a series of questions and led the poor fellow down a road of complete embarrassment. The speaker knew how to "go for the jugular," and he did it well.

Eights may champion the truly vulnerable as a way of dealing with their own hidden vulnerability. Underneath the rugged exterior of the strong Eight minister is a tender person who must guard his or her own vulnerability.

The church needs Eights who will not be afraid to speak their minds and go against the stream. At the same time, Eights can overlook the subtleties that are an everyday part of ministry. It may take a trusted friend to pull an Eight aside and inform him or her that "they just stomped on somebody's emotional tulips."

Eight ministers are sometimes not aware of other people's emotional needs. They think that since they do not have these needs, surely others do not.

The movement toward wholeness for the Eight is in the direction of the Two, the Sheltering Servant. This Two style of relating is needed to balance the strength and assertiveness of the Eight.

While Eights fear dependency, they need to realize that in order to truly care, one must risk independence and involve oneself in the complexities of caring relationships that might involve vulnerability. The minister who is an Eight needs to acknowledge that his or her power is sometimes overwhelming to others. Growth comes when the Eight attempts to get in touch with the tenderness that comes from the Two side of life. It is buried within them.

If it were not for these Powerful Prophets, the institutional church would probably never be reformed. To say that Martin Luther was an Eight is an understatement. His namesake, Martin Luther King, Jr., was also a healthy Eight who mixed power with relational skills. Such ministers who risk much to get their way are needed in a church that often seeks a status quo existence.

Type Nine: The Need to Avoid Conflict (The Mediator)

The Peaceful Pastor

The Nine minister is perhaps the stereotype that has been used by television and Hollywood most often to portray the parson. This figure is rather passive and lame, more of a background figure to the main characters in the drama. The parson tends to go along with the status quo and not upset the applecart. This is not a strong figure and can be depended on to provide just enough needed assurance for the rituals of life. Bring the parson in for the needed service, and then ship him out and get on with real life.

In the real world of the church, there are many Nine ministers. These people are peacemakers and compromisers. They tend to go along with the way things are but can be counted on to be a calm presence. They offer a quiet assurance that many people need. They will not command respect but are often given respect because of their office. Type Nine ministers will avoid conflict at all costs.

They do not have a strong sense of self and are comfortable in an institution like the church, which tends to define one's identity. This nebulous sense of self, which comes from childhood origins, requires that identity be gained from a close environment.

Nines are usually very pastoral and project a sense of serenity. It may be hard to get them to make a decision. They tend to lean on congregational structures in the decision-making process.

The movement toward wholeness for the Nine is in the direction of the Three, the Successful Shepherd. This movement will help Nines learn to value their own identity and help them risk asserting themselves. Nines need to learn to face conflict and negative feelings in order to gain strength.

Nines can be wonderful comforters since they offer such a peaceful presence, although it might be hard for parishioners to know who they really are. When Nines become more balanced with the best part of the assertive Three, the combination makes for a more powerful, peaceful pastor.

When first becoming familiar with the Enneagram, it is common to think that you are a combination of several numbers. The theory maintains that a person can only be one number. The various complexities within a given number comes from a concept called "the wings," which states that each number has some of the number immediately next to it on the Enneagram circle. Usually one of the adjacent numbers is the dominant wing and greatly determines the nature of the compulsive type. For instance, I am a Four/Three, which means that I am a Four with a Three wing. This mixture makes for a fairly creative individualist with strong achievement needs.

Knowing one's Enneagram number takes some time. Since each person has some qualities and weaknesses from each of the numbers, it is not so easy to label ourselves. After all, we are not numbers. The numbers are simply offered as a model to help us discover the bindings that are keeping us from truly seeing ourselves and our world in a less compulsive way.

The following bibliography lists an inventory you can take to help discover your number. Inventories help, but the best way to discover who you really are is to listen to all the types and then struggle with which one honestly describes you.

Enneagram Bibliography

For particular attention:

To discover your personality type or number, the most user-friendly book is Don Riso's *Discovering Your Personality Type: The Enneagram Questionnaire*. Boston/New York: Houghton Mifflin Co., 1992.

To set the Enneagram in the Christian context and biblical perspective, a good book is Richard Rhor and Andreas Ebert's *Discovering the Enneagram: An Ancient Tool for a New Spiritual Journey*. New York: Crossroad, 1990.

The basic text I have used for understanding the Enneagram is Don Riso's *Personality Types: Using the Enneagram for Self-Discovery*. Boston/New York: Houghton Mifflin Co., 1987.

A good book for a fairly simple explanation of the Enneagram in readable language is Kathleen Hurley and Theodore Dobson's, *What's My Type*. San Francisco: Harper, 1991.

To use the Enneagram in spiritual direction, a good book is Suzanne Zuercher's *Enneagram Companions*. Notre Dame, Ind.: Ave Maria Press, 1993.

Other books:

Bergen, Ellis, and Fitzgerald, Eddie. *An Enneagram Guide: A Spirituality of Love in Brokenness*. Dublin, Ireland: Twenty Third Publications, 1993.

Hurley, Kathleen V., and Dobson, Theodore E. *My Best Self: Using the Enneagram to Free the Soul*. San Francisco: Harper San Francisco, 1993.

Kelly, Mary Helen. *Skin Deep: Designer Clothes by God*. Memphis: Monastery of St. Claire, 1990.

Keys, Margaret Frings. *Emotions and the Enneagram*. Muir Beach, Calif.: Molysdatur Publications, 1992.

Metz, Barbara, and Burchill, John. *The Enneagram and Prayer: Discovering Our True Selves Before God*. Denville, N.J.: Dimension Books, Inc., 1987.

Nogosek, Robert J. *Nine Portraits of Jesus: Discovering Jesus*

Through the Enneagram. Denville, N.J.: Dimension Books, Inc., 1987.

Olson, Robert W. *Stepping Out Within: A Practical Guide to Personality Types, Relationships and Self-Transformation.* San Juan Capistrano, Calif.: Awakened Press, 1993.

Palmer, Helen. *The Enneagram: Understanding Yourself and Others in Your Life.* San Francisco: Harper & Row Pulbishers, 1988.

Riso, Don Richard. *Understanding the Enneagram: The Practical Guide to Personality Types.* Boston/New York: Houghton Mufflin Co., 1990.

Riso, Don Richard. *Enneagram Transformations: Releases and Affirmations for Healing Your Personality Type.* Boston/New York: Houghton Mufflin Co., 1993.

Tickerhoof, Bernard. *Conversion and the Enneagram: Transformation of the Self in Christ.* Denville, N.J.: Dimension Books, 1991.

Zuercher, Suzanne. *Enneagram Spirituality.* Notre Dame, Ind.: Ave Maria Press, 1992.

Part III

A Twenty-One-Day Spiritual Renewal Journey for Ministers

Introduction to the Journey

We are meant to be pilgrims on life's journey, not simply tourists. A pilgrim is looking for something and attempts to follow a certain path. A tourist is looking at the sights.

Jesus was on a pilgrimage. As part of that pilgrimage, he journeyed into the wilderness. He knew that only in the lonely places would he be able to face the needed time of testing and find a time of reflection.

Even Jesus had to have these times of coming home to himself. Many of those who wanted to follow him did not understand his need to be alone. They were always wanting a little more of him.

Ministers know the feeling of people wanting a part of us. It comes with the job description. What we do not do very well is take times of renewal so that we will have something to give.

The journey I wish to offer you now is somewhat like an invitation to go back to the town in which you spent your childhood years. I want you to go back to places of origin and visit some sacred shrines from your past journey. Do not view them as a tourist, for these are from your story and your past.

Some will be places of illumination and joy, and some might be places of pain and darkness. We learn by reflecting on both places.

I want for you to sit at the emotional soda fountain and remember the past. The Bible is often read as a past-tense story. When we preach from its pages, we hope that the scriptural story will take on a present-tense meaning for the people to whom we are speaking. We hope that by remembering the past, our congregations will see their own stories in *the* story.

I am asking you now to reflect on your story in the light of the need for renewal. When we remember our own stories and those places of light and darkness, we can ask God to look over our shoulders as we walk backwards.

Most ministers remind me of that old Gatorade commercial in which a sweaty athlete, who looks as if he is on the losing end of things, looks to his opponent and says, "It looks like you could use some Gatorade." The implication is that the one speaking needs to hit the bottle but is projecting the need onto his opponent.

Ministers are constantly called upon to stand before others and lead them in times of reflection and renewal. Some of the people we serve could surely use some "Gatorade," but in our hearts, we know that, sometimes even more than our people, we need our own cup of cold water.

I have attempted to show in the first part of this book the reality that caring for others takes its personal toll. The yoke of Christ is easy only because he is in the yoke with us. We so often attempt to carry this yoke as if we are alone.

The Enneagram has been offered as a tool for self-study and spiritual guidance. Using the Enneagram is one way for ministers to break through the "crust" that often forms around us while we do ministry and live life. The image of God within us is often covered over, even as we do God's work.

I invite you now to take this twenty-one-day journey. Find a specific time each day and commit that time to these exercises. This journey is offered to some as a beginning. To others it will simply be part of your continuing journey of exercising spiritual disciplines.

Each day a portion of the scriptural story will be highlighted. As you read it, do not let it lead you down the path of the last sermon you preached on the text. This time, let the words from *the* story speak to *your* story. This time, you are not talking to other pilgrims; you are remembering that you are a pilgrim.

The Renewal Journey

DAY 1

Being a Child of God

Focus: "I am fearfully and wonderfully made."

Where can I go from your spirit?
    Or where can I flee from your presence?
If I ascend to heaven, you are there;
    if I make my bed in Sheol, you are there.
If I take the wings of the morning
    and settle at the farthest limits of the sea,
even there your hand shall lead me,
    and your right hand shall hold me fast.
If I say, "Surely the darkness shall cover me,
    and the light around me become night,"
even the darkness is not dark to you;
    the night is as bright as the day,
    for darkness is as light to you.

For it was you who formed my inward parts;
    you knit me together in my mother's womb.
I praise you, for I am fearfully and wonderfully made.
    Wonderful are your works;
that I know very well.
    My frame was not hidden from you,
when I was being made in secret,
    intricately woven in the depths of the earth.
Your eyes beheld my unformed substance.
In your book were written
    all the days that were formed for me,
    when none of them as yet existed.

—Psalm 139:7-16[1]

Today, as you begin your journey, try to remember the first time you felt like you were a child of God. It is important for ministers to remember that we are persons first and ministers second.

Who first brought you to this reality of your "childhood"? Was it a parent, a Sunday school teacher, a friend, or an occasion that pointed you to the idea that you were God's?

Underneath your "uniform," you are God's child. Your role, even though it is religious, can cover up this reality.

Picture the moment in your mind, the scene when you first knew you were God's child. Make this scene very detailed. Who is there? What is around you? How old are you? Are you in a room? near a lake or mountain? Were there certain words or actions that caused you to feel God's claiming of you? Did a person claim you and make you feel like it was God claiming you?

You may not always be an ordained minister. You will always be a child of God.

End your time with five minutes of silence. Simply begin your silence with the affirmation "O God, I am your child". . . and wait.

DAY 2

Come As a child

Focus: "I bent down to [you] and fed [you]."

When Israel was a child, I loved him,
> and out of Egypt I called my son.
The more I called them,
> the more they went from me;
they kept sacrificing to the Baals,
> and offering incense to idols.

Yet it was I who taught Ephraim to walk,
> I took them up in my arms;
> but they did not know that I healed them.
I led them with cords of human kindness,

with bands of love.
I was to them like those
who lift infants to their cheeks.
I bent down to them and fed them.
—Hosea 11:1-4

Ministry is so serious. Today think of your favorite childhood game. With whom did you play the game? Was there a special place of play for you? Did your play involve risk, novelty, winning, loosing? Try to remember what it felt like to play as a child.

Remember the most tender moment of your childhood. Was it leaning against your mother's breast while being comforted? What is the picture that comes to your mind when you think of being held?

God wants us to come as children. How do you do that now? What part of your life and ministry needs to be more childlike? What part does play have in your life now?

In these next five minutes, plan a time of play to happen in the week ahead. Reflect on the space you have in your life for true recreation.

DAY 3

Coming Home

Focus: "A journey to a distant country"

The Scripture text is the story of the prodigal son in Luke 15:11-32. Remember the son who journeyed to a far country and the son who stayed home.

In your growing-up years, were you the stay-at-home type or the one who "journeyed" to your own far country?

Are you glad that you stayed home? Where would the far country have been for you? If you journeyed to a far country, do you regret it? What did you learn out there? Where is home for you now?

In your time now, go back to a home. It can be a place, or it can be a home that you need. Go back there. Sit on the front porch or back steps or under a tree. Know that God waits for you "at home" no matter how grown up you have become.

Finish your time today by focusing on where a home place or a home base is for you daily. You need a home place within yourself.

DAY 4

The Knowledge of God

Focus: "A spirit of wisdom and understanding"

The spirit of the LORD shall rest on him,
the spirit of wisdom and understanding,
the spirit of counsel and might,
the spirit of knowledge and the fear of the LORD
His delight shall be in the fear of the LORD.
He shall not judge by what his eyes see,
  or decide by what his ears hear.

—Isaiah 11:2-3

Today focus on that time when you can first remember learning about God. Was it from a parent, a Sunday school teacher, an occasion of joy or sorrow? What was the image of God that first formed in your mind?

Where along your journey have you had times of crisis in your knowing about God? When did you have to "let go of childish things" in order to "know"? Was it in adolescence, in college, or did your challenge come in seminary or later? How did you deal with this challenge to your knowledge about God? What effect has your journey in knowing about God had on you?

What place does knowledge have in your present understanding about God? What has most influenced your knowing? What is it that you must know now in order to believe?

In your remaining time, write your affirmation of faith. Be honest. Write no more than what you feel is necessary and really believe.

After you have finished writing this affirmation, read it slowly and deliberately to yourself, allowing God to overhear your reading. Now, read it aloud and listen. What is it that you need to know in order to believe?

DAY 5

The Call to Ministry

Focus: "For you shall go to all to whom I send you."

Now the word of the LORD came to me saying,
   "Before I formed you in the womb I knew you,
   and before you were born I consecrated you;
   I appointed you a prophet to the nations."
Then I said, "Ah, Lord GOD! Truly I do not know how to
speak, for I am only a boy." But the LORD said to me,
   "Do not say 'I am only a boy';
   for you shall go to all to whom I send you,
   and you shall speak whatever I command you.'
                                          —Jeremiah 1:4-7

This is the day on your journey when you are asked to focus
on that time in your life when your personhood became envel-
oped into God's call to ministry. Your call may have been a very
explicit experience, or it may have been a slow tugging of your
life toward ministry. This part of your journey is a time to
remember what got you going on this road called ministry.

Find a quiet place and clear your mind. Some pilgrims find it
helpful to have some meditative music playing to help still the
mind.

Slowly . . . very slowly, put together the picture of your call.
If it was a particular place and time, make some effort to picture
the place in a very specific and real way. Ask God to help you
relive the moment as much as possible. Feel the feelings. Remember the emotions, the smiles, the tears, the anxiety, the fear,
the hopes, the questions.

If your call was more stretched out, take some time to identify
the turning points that caused you to change direction. Were
these points people, incidents, books, or other signs along your
way?

How long ago was your call? Does your call need renewing?
Like a library book that is worth keeping in order to finish
reading, so your call may need renewing.

You cannot relive the past, but the power of the past can come across the years to you. It is one of the miracles of God to receive grace and power from the past.

In your closing moments of the journey today, ask God to bring your calling back to you. Remember your call.

DAY 6

Resistance to the Call

Focus: "But Jonah set out to flee from the presence of the Lord."

> Now the word of the LORD came to Jonah son of Amittai, saying, "Go at once to Nineveh, that great city, and cry out against it; for their wickedness has come up before me." But Jonah set out to flee to Tarshish from the presence of the LORD. He went down to Joppa and found a ship going to Tarshish; so he paid his fare and went on board, to go with them to Tarshish away from the presence of the LORD" (Jonah 1:1-3).

Resistance is often a part of the call of God. Various biblical characters offered resistance to God's call. Moses tried to tell God that he could not speak well enough. Jeremiah claimed to be too young. Jonah had other plans for his life.

Resistance has a place in the struggle to follow God's call. It is through resistance that we become strong. Resistance can be one of the best teachers. It can be a time of testing somewhat akin to the physical conditioning an athlete undergoes in preparation for a competition.

Did you offer resistance to God's call? What happened in that resistance?

In what moments of your life have you found excuses for not claiming God's call to you? In what moments have you wanted to, or actually did, run from God's call?

God's call is always accompanied by an anointing, so that the person called will not be without the means to accomplish the bidding of the call. In what forms has your anointing come? Do you need to discover again the anointing?

In your closing moments today, offer to God your resistance.

If that resistance is in the past, bring it back into your memory and reflect on what it has taught you. Your resistance has helped make you what you are today.

If you are still struggling with God's call, offer to God the resistance you presently have. Name it. Picture your resistance on a turntable; see it from all sides. What does the resistance mean? What is God saying to you through the resistance?

Offer to God your resistance and ask for the gift of discernment, so that you might better understand the meaning of your resistance. Close your time today with the Serenity Prayer: "God, grant me the serenity to accept the things I cannot change, the courage to change the things I can, and the wisdom to know the difference."

DAY 7

Sabbath

Focus: "Being and doing"

> Now as they went on their way, he entered a certain village, where a woman named Martha welcomed him into her home. She had a sister named Mary, who sat at the Lord's feet and listened to what he was saying. But Martha was distracted by her many tasks; so she came to him and asked, "Lord, do you not care that my sister has left me to do all the work by myself? Tell her then to help me." But the Lord answered her, "Martha, Martha, you are worried and distracted by many things; there is need of only one thing. Mary has chosen the better part, which will not be taken away from her" (Luke 10:38-42).

A person once said to me, "When you are what you do, when you don't, you aren't." Today reflect on who you are when you are not doing ministry. What are you apart from your role as minister?

Today is a place of stopping along your journey. The only thing you are asked to do today is "be." What will that mean for you? Do you know how to "be"? Is it hard for you to simply "be"?

In your allotted time today, just "be" . . . whatever that means for you. If you need some help, below is a simple way to step toward "being." Repeat this familiar Scripture text from Psalm 46:10, but this time drop off a phrase each time you repeat it.

"Be still, and know that I am God!"

"Be still, and know that I am . . ."

"Be still, and know . . ."

"Be still . . . "

"Be . . . "

DAY 8

Remembering Your Mother: The Church

Focus: "I derived much comfort and joy from your love."

For you are receiving the outcome of your faith, the salvation of your souls. Concerning this salvation, the prophets who prophesied of the grace that was to be yours made careful search and inquiry (1 Peter 1:9-10).

When I remember you in my prayers, I always thank my God because I hear of your love for all the saints and your faith toward the Lord Jesus. I pray that the sharing of your faith may become effective when you perceive all the good that we may do for Christ. I have indeed received much joy and encouragement from your love, because the hearts of the saints have been refreshed through you, my brother (Philemon 4-7).

Today is a day for embracing what the church has meant to you. The church has often been called "mother." How has the church nurtured you?

Dig into your past and remember days of vacation Bible school, children's choirs, acolyte duties, or leaning down behind some tall person's head in front of you so the minister would not see you go to sleep during the sermon.

For you, the church may have been a good mother, offering you the first milk of faith. For you, the church may have been a judgmental mother, offering rules and guilt. Was the church

ever manipulative? Do you, in this moment, need to thank
mother church or forgive mother church?

Our mothers and fathers were our first "gods." We saw life
through them. They were life-givers in the godlike roles of
creators. Since parent figures are not gods, it is important that
we come to see them as ones who made mistakes. They were
not perfect in their loving.

In your closing moments, reflect on what it has meant for you
to have the church as mother. Are you still looking to the church
as a mother? Are you expecting too much or too little? Sometimes we need the church in the wrong ways. We may end up
resenting "mother" church for not giving us what we need.

Wait before God with this image of "mother" church and see
what happens.

DAY 9

Testing the Spirits

Focus: "Do not believe every spirit."

Beloved, do not believe every spirit, but test the spirits to
see whether they are from God; for many false prophets
have gone out into the world. By this you know the Spirit
of God: every spirit that confesses that Jesus Christ has
come in the flesh is from God, and every spirit that does
not confess Jesus is not from God. And this is the spirit of
the antichrist, of which you have heard that it is coming;
and now it is already in the world. Little children, you are
from God, and have conquered them; for the one who is in
you is greater than the one who is in the world. They are
from the world; therefore what they say is from the world,
and the world listens to them. We are from God. Whoever
knows God listens to us, and whoever is not from God does
not listen to us. From this we know the spirit of truth and
the spirit of error (1 John 4:1-6).

Some of the people you serve as minister may think of you as
a Moses-like figure who routinely talks to God face-to-face. You
may be trusted, oftentimes, because people think you have a

direct line to God.

The truth is that you struggle in your own way with keeping the lines of communication open. You, too, have to test the spirits. All that comes your way, even though you are called of God, is not of God.

Those of us who deal constantly with the spirit world are in danger of listening to powerful voices that come in deceptive and often attractive tones. Wrapped up in our efforts to remain effective are the voices of ego and power. Ego and power can become baptized and take on the face of the Divine. Caution is needed.

We only need to look to either side to see one of our own who has not effectively discerned the spirits. Television screens are filled with the smiling faces of smooth-talking ministers who have confused the spirits.

What is driving you? What has control of your life that is not of God? Have you used your role as minister to excuse your misuse of power?

In your closing time today, ask for the power of discernment. Ask God to help you perceive clearly the spiritual powers at work in your life.

It may help for you to write down that which claims you. After you have written down various items, pray over them and begin the task of discerning the spirits. Sometimes too much of a good thing can become a bad thing. What on your list has too much control of you?

DAY 10

Bread for the Journey

Focus: "Protect them from the evil one."

"I am asking on their behalf; I am not asking on behalf of the world, but on behalf of those whom you gave me, because they are yours. All mine are yours, and yours are mine; and I have been glorified in them. And now I am no longer in the world, but they are in the world, and I am coming to you. Holy Father, protect them in your name that you have given me, so that they may be one, as we are one. . . . I am not asking you to take them out of the world, but I ask you to protect them from the evil one" (John 17:9-11, 15).

Today is a day to take stock of your resources for the journey. This is your inventory, so be honest.

How much time each day do you allow for prayer? Do you have a set time of day to pray? Do you have a place for prayer? What books are like old friends to you that assist you in your journey?

Do you read the Bible each day just for you and not for sermon preparation or for teaching purposes? How do you feel about the Bible? Has it become too familiar to you? Are you able to hear its words?

Where is the temperance in your life? To what can you point to remind you of discipline? Do you have a regular exercise pattern? Are you disciplined about your body, or is your body a reflection of your lax spirit?

Do you devote adequate time to your family? Has the church or your job become your "lover" instead of a love? Are you having an affair with your work?

What are you doing as a servant that is not part of your job? In other words, what acts of mercy are you doing that are not required by your work?

Today try to answer these questions honestly in the presence of God. Do not be hard on yourself. God already knows the answers to these questions.

God's love is assured for you, but some of the answers to these questions may reflect an uncertainty about self-love. What are you still trying to prove? Are you hiding?

Reflect on the resources for your journey.

DAY 11

Education for Ministry

Focus: "Learn from me."

I will instruct you and teach you the way you should go;
I will counsel you with my eye upon you.
—Psalm 32:8

"Take my yoke upon you, and learn from me; for I am gentle and humble in heart, and you will find rest for your souls" (Matthew 11:29).

Today is a time for reflecting on the question, Am I enrolled in the school of Christian living?

What are you doing to keep from becoming stale? What books have you read recently? How many days last year did you spend in continuing education? How are you presently learning about God? Have you explored new ways to pray?

If you are a parish minister, what do you do to keep your sermon preparation time fresh and alive? Who is the best preacher you have ever heard? Why?

Beyond books and seminars, what do you think Jesus meant when he said, "Learn from me"? What does this now mean for you and your ministry? What is the latest thing you have learned from Jesus?

Close your time today with this sentence prayer: "Lord, what do you need to teach me?"

DAY 12

Temptations

Focus: "In the wilderness . . . and famished"

Jesus, full of the Holy Spirit, returned from the Jordan and was led by the Spirit in the wilderness, where for forty days he was tempted by the devil. He ate nothing at all during those days, and when they were over, he was famished (Luke 4:1-3a).

Temptations abound in ministry. The primary temptation is to take ourselves too seriously. God smiled when you were made. Everybody is strange in a different way, especially ministers!

Today is a time for you to follow the One who called you, to follow him into the wilderness. Consider again Jesus' own temptations, but put your primary temptations in place of the ones he faced.

Ministers spend a lot of time hiding. Some of those we serve think we are above temptations. Today embrace your particular humanness. Some of the same drives that make you an effective minister can also lead you into temptation. You must name these drives before you can tame them.

In your closing time, name your temptations. Speak them into reality, and offer them to God rather than spending more energy in hiding.

Imagine that all your temptations are in one drawer. Open the drawer and place the temptations on top of the desk. What can you and God do with them?

DAY 13

Water into Wine: Remembering Success

Focus: "He revealed his glory and his disciples believed."

When the steward tasted the water that had become wine, and did not know where it came from (though the servants who had drawn the water knew), the steward called the bridegroom and said to him, "Everyone serves the good wine first, and then the inferior wine after the guests have become drunk. But you have kept the good wine until now." Jesus did this, the first of his signs, in Cana of Galilee, and revealed his glory; and his disciples believed in him (John 2:9-11).

Today is a day of celebration. Call to mind what you believe to be the successes of your ministry.

Walk back to the feelings around one of those successful moments. What made the success happen? Was it hard work? Was it because of grace?

Is most of your success focused on individual people or on programs? What was your last success?

Is being successful important to you? Does that question bother you or get in your way? Do you need to let go of the need to be successful in order to enjoy life more?

If God were watching a video collage of your successes, which ones would cause God to clap?

In closing, pick one successful time. Hold it up like a snapshot. Thank God for it. What difference has the success made in your life or in the lives of others? Look closely at the snapshot. In your own way, close your time with a prayer of thanksgiving for the success and for the gift that you are in God's creation.

DAY 14

Facing Fear with Jesus

Focus: "Do not be afraid."

"So have no fear of them; for nothing is covered up that will not be uncovered, and nothing secret that will not become known. What I say to you in the dark, tell in the light; and what you hear whispered, proclaim from the housetops. Do not fear those who kill the body but cannot kill the soul; rather fear him who can destroy both soul and body in hell. Are not two sparrows sold for a penny? Yet not one of them will fall to the ground apart from your Father. And even the hairs of your head are all counted. So do not be afraid; you are of more value than many sparrows" (Matthew 10:26-31).

As you read the guided meditation below, try to "be" it.

You are sitting beside a small lake. There is a red maple tree beside the lake that provides a slight bit of shade. Gently lean over and look into the lake. It is calm and still. You can see the reflection of your face clearly.

Now, picture next to your reflection the thing you fear most in life. Make it real. If it is a thought, give it some form. Look at it in the water. How does looking at its form beside your form make you feel?

As you are looking into the water, you hear someone come up behind you, but before you have the chance to turn around, you notice the person lean over your stooped frame. You see the face of this person also reflected in the water beside your fear and beside you.

The face is the face of Jesus. His hand is resting on your

shoulder. As he looks into the water and into your face and your fear, he whispers, "Do not be afraid."

Listen . . . Wait . . . Be with Jesus and your fear.

DAY 15

Remembering Your Power

Focus: "All authority in heaven and on earth . . . given"

Now the eleven disciples went to Galilee, to the mountain to which Jesus had directed them. When they saw him, they worshiped him; but some doubted. And Jesus came and said to them, "All authority in heaven and on earth has been given to me. Go therefore and make disciples of all nations, baptizing them in the name of the Father and of the Son and of the Holy Spirit, and teaching them to obey everything that I have commanded you. And remember, I am with you always, to the end of the age" (Matthew 28:16-20).

Ministers are allowed to stand in very sacred places. You are invited to be present when few others are given access.

Children are "given" to you that you might bestow a baptismal blessing. You have walked into hospital rooms where the sign reads "no visitors." You have looked into the eyes of the husband or wife who confesses to you about the other love in his or her life when no one else knows.

In a day when it is hard to get anyone's attention without doing something spectacular, you are allowed to have twenty minutes or so to make a point. People who will not give some others the time of day come to listen to you.

You offer words of sacred covenant to two starry-eyed lovers who are certain that they will be joined together forever. While others remain silent around an open grave, your words are spoken into their silence.

"All authority in heaven and on earth" has been given to you. Even though a secular world makes fun of the power of ministry and portrays our character as Milquetoast, there is power in what we do.

Today remember the power you have been given. It can be a strange power. Sometimes this power is perceived as weakness, but it is power.

Remember today that the Christ who bestows this power on you is the only one who truly understands its nature. The world often does not comprehend this kind of power you have in your grasp. It is the power of heaven and earth.

Hold that power gently in your hands this very moment. Does it feel heavy? light? Do you feel it?

As you close your time, ask God to help you embrace and better understand the power you have been given.

DAY 16

Remembering a Misuse of Power

Focus: "You are the man!"

Nathan said to David, "You are the man! Thus says the LORD, the God of Israel: I anointed you king over Israel, and I rescued you from the hand of Saul; I gave you your master's house, and your master's wives into your bosom, and gave you the house of Israel and of Judah; and if that had been too little, I would have added as much more. Why have you despised the word of the LORD, to do what is evil in his sight? You have struck down Uriah the Hittite with the sword, and have taken his wife to be your wife, and have killed him with the sword of the Ammonites" (2 Samuel 12:7-9).

Today is a day to face the shadow side of your personality. It is time to remember those times when you have misused the power that has been given to you. It is time to observe and let go.

Have you misused the power of the pulpit? Have you at times offered your personal agenda rather than the Word of the Lord? Have you been angry at your people from the pulpit? Have you denied them God's grace because you did not have any use for them or felt they did not deserve it? Have you misused money that was given to you in good faith?

Did you at some time step over the boundary in a counseling relationship? Did you inappropriately step through the doorway of intimacy that was opened to you because of your own vulnerability?

Like King David, have you insulated yourself from the correcting love of God for you? Did the privilege of ministry cover up the obligation of ministry?

Today be honest with God about times you have misused your power. Like an old video or home movie that you have hidden away and would rather not see, pull the moment out. Watch what you did, but this time allow Jesus to sit beside you.

Jesus was there when you misused the power. He is with you now. Ask this Lord you serve to help you understand the reasons why you stepped over the line.

Make a promise to yourself and to God that you will seek professional help if you feel you cannot control something in your life that has led you to the misuse of your power. You can make a new beginning. We all need help at some time in our lives. Remember that the physician who has himself for a patient has a fool for a doctor.

Close your time with some deep, cleansing breaths. God wishes to offer you renewal and absolution.

DAY 17

The Need for Forgiveness

Focus: "Forgiving little, loving little"

"Therefore, I tell you, her sins, which were many, have been forgiven; hence she has shown great love. But the one to whom little is forgiven, loves little" (Luke 7:47).

No matter what your denominational affiliation is, you are a dispenser of absolution. Everybody needs forgiveness sometime in his or her life. Oftentimes, people may have looked to you to offer a word of absolution. Have you been able to give it?

Now is the time for you to receive it. It is time to weep over your sins, so that you can be given absolution. What are you hiding?

It is time to look into the face of your Master, but this time do not ask for help for someone you serve. Ask God to help *you*.

If you feel that you do not need forgiveness, then open the back corners of your soul because the need is there. Look into the face of Jesus.

You have spoken about that face of love; now see it for yourself. As you look into the face of this Christ, he asks you this question: "(*Your name*), for what do you need my forgiveness?"

He waits. Tell him now. It is time to be free.

DAY 18

The Wounds of Ministry

Focus: "Why is my wound incurable?"

Your words were found, and I ate them,
    and your words became to me a joy
    and the delight of my heart;
for I am called by your name,
    O LORD, God of hosts.
I did not sit in the company of merrymakers,
    nor did I rejoice;
under the weight of your hand I sat alone,
    for you had filled me with indignation.
Why is my pain unceasing,
    my wound incurable,
    refusing to be healed?
Truly, you are to me like a deceitful brook,
    like waters that fail.

        —Jeremiah 15:16-18

Many ministers are among the walking wounded. Someone once said that ministers tend to shoot their own wounded. I have found that ministers, as a whole, are a very judgmental group of professionals.

If you are reading this, you are probably one of the wounded. Most of us are. I am one of them. Some of my wounds I will share with no one. Some I need to share with someone. God knows all of them.

What are your wounds that have come from being in ministry?

Who has hurt you? Have you felt passed over professionally? Even though you were called to be a humble servant, have you felt like you have been slighted? Have you had to put up with low pay, unsatisfactory housing, poor office space, and so on? Have you felt guilty for even thinking of these kinds of things when you have been called to be a servant? If you do, then know that guilt is a wound. It is time to be honest about your wounds.

Have you at times wounded yourself? Have you reached out to someone sexually in an inappropriate manner? Have you become emotionally lazy because those around you do not seem to care? Have you contributed to your own woundedness?

Do you sometimes feel like Jeremiah, who often felt the need to complain to God about being in God's service? Now is your "free space in bingo." Now is the time of lamentation. Go ahead, complain. For everything there is a season. Now is your time.

Offer to God your wounds—those that have been inflicted upon you and those you have brought on yourself. Write down these wounds if it will help to see them. If you do write them, after you have offered them to God, stand in front of a fire or garbage can, rip up the paper, and cast it into the fire or the garbage. Go ahead, that is what God does if these wounds are weighing us down.

God honors those other wounds in which you felt pain not brought on by your own doing. If you cannot tear them up or throw them away, then wait for tomorrow. Tomorrow will be a time for healing.

You are loved, wounds and all, complaints and all. The wounded Christ will now put his arms around you. You are his servant—his wounded servant.

DAY 19

A Time for Healing

Focus: "Touching the fringe of his clothes"

As he went, the crowds pressed in on him. Now there was a woman who had been suffering from hemorrhages for twelve years; and though she had spent all she had on physicians, no one could cure her. She came up behind him and touched the fringe of his clothes, and immediately her hemorrhage stopped. Then Jesus asked, "Who touched me?" When all denied it, Peter said, "Master, the crowds surround you and press in on you." But Jesus said, "Someone touched me; for I noticed that power had gone out from me." When the woman saw that she could not remain hidden, she came trembling; and falling down before him, she declared in the presence of all the people why she had touched him, and how she had been immediately healed. He said to her, "Daughter, your faith has made you well; go in peace" (Luke 8:42b-48).

Those of us who stand before "the crowds" know what it means to look into the faces of those who say they have "come seeking Jesus." We know that some are there knowing what they need, while others come out of habit or custom or needs for control and power. The crowd has no real identity, but individuals in the crowd do have a particular story and specific needs.

The woman in Luke's story was, in fact, part of the crowd. What separated her from the rest was her struggling faith mixed with risk. She felt that if she could only touch the fringe of this man's clothes, perhaps some leftover power might rub off.

She made no noise. She asked no questions. She was only one among many. Her wound was shameful. It rendered her unclean according to the religious norms of the day; and yet Jesus felt her touch more than that of any other person in the crowd that was pressing in on him. Her touch made her a person to Jesus.

You, who are a person before you are a minister, are part of the crowd. This Jesus has felt your presence in the midst of all the others. He knows of your wounds. He has been listening as you have taken your journey. He now waits for you to reach out to him.

It is time for healing. Do you want to be healed? Are you ready to step out in your need? You cannot be healed if you do not reach out in acknowledgment of your wounds.

When Jesus looked at that daughter of Israel long ago, it was a look of love that completed her healing. Her unwavering faith met the reaching eyes of a Savior who loved her and her wound. It is now your time.

Read the Scripture again. This time place yourself in the crowd. You are the wounded minister reaching out from all the people. Those people include other ministers. The crowd is made up also of the people you serve. They are all important, but just now you are alone in the crowd. Jesus has singled you out.

Listen to his question, "Who touched me?" Answer the question. Be ready to offer him your wound. It is time for healing.

Feel his power, a power you have often proclaimed for others. Now the power is for you. Feel the power flowing toward you. Let it fill the empty places. Let it touch the hurting places.

It is time for healing . . . for you.

DAY 20

The Need for Renewal

Focus: "Do you love me?"

When they had finished breakfast, Jesus said to Simon Peter, "Simon son of John, do you love me more than these?" He said to him, "Yes, Lord; you know that I love you." Jesus said to him, "Feed my lambs" (John 21:15).

Somewhere in your past, you responded to the call of the One who asked you to step though the fog and join him on the shore. He had earlier asked you to fish for people.

Some days the catch was good. On other days the nets came up empty, and so did you. There have been times when you have not even cast the nets. You either felt it would do no good or you were simply tired, physically or emotionally.

You may have progressed from a small boat to a larger one. You may have remained in the small boat either by choice or by circumstance. The waters may have been productive, or they may have been shallow and rather empty of fish.

In some moments you have felt companionship in the boat. In other times you have felt the loneliness of fishing. You have been praised for your efforts and criticized. Some days the sailing was smooth; other days the storms seemed endless.

But today you hear his call again. The voice is familiar, although it may have been some time since you have heard it in this way. Today he asks you to step from the boat and sit down by the fire.

Today the fishing is over. He wants to feed you. He wants to serve you. He knows of your proud moments when you claimed him, and he knows of your times of denial. He still needs you. He remembers when he called you and your answer.

Today he has but one question. The question is not original. He asked it long ago to another caster of nets whom he loved greatly and whom he needed to help carry on the fishing.

"Do you love me?" That is the question. He knows that you will have to love him if you are to continue the fishing. He knows about empty nets and shallow waters. He knows of denials and the calls you receive from other shores.

"Do you love me?" He knows that there have been times when it was hard for you to love him. There have been times when the storms have been more frequent than the still waters. He knows that you have at times wanted to fish other seas than the ones he offered. He knows.

Now he is preparing to serve you. He wants to offer you a time of refreshment. He wants you to know that he knows and cares. In this moment, the moments of your failures become the coals for the fire. He consumes them in the fire of his preparation.

All he wants to know is the answer to the one question. As he prepares to serve you, the question hangs in the air. Let him serve you. Let him restore you.

On another day you will be asked to fish again, but today he wants to feed you. He wants you to be nourished so that you can answer the question.

Before you answer, look into those eyes—those same eyes that knew you when you were called, those same eyes that saw your mother hold you in moments you do not remember. Look into those eyes and see his love for you. It is a special love—the love reserved for those who try to mend nets and pilot boats and catch fish.

Spend this moment with him. Let him feed you. Then answer his question.

DAY 21

A Revisioning of Ministry

Focus: "Follow me."

As he walked by the Sea of Galilee, he saw two brothers, Simon, who is called Peter, and Andrew his brother, casting a net into the sea—for they were fishermen. And he said to them, "Follow me, and I will make you fish for people." Immediately they left their nets and followed him (Matthew 4:18-20).

It is time for you to end this part of your journey, but then there is the new beginning. Those first fishermen Jesus called discovered that as one journey ended, another began.

What did you leave to follow Jesus into ministry? What empty nets were left hanging to dry as you stepped off the boat of the past and onto the path he offered?

Something is always left behind when a person is asked to follow Jesus. It has to be that way. Much is gained by listening to the One who says, "Follow me." It is time to remember what has been gained.

Today Jesus wants you to remember all those who have felt the net close in around them because you cast the net their way. You will never know some of the occasions in which people were "caught" because of your casting. You are not supposed to know. It is just that way—his way.

There is to be no lining up of fish at the end of the day as if you were coming in from a tourist fishing trip. You are not a tourist. You are a pilgrim who has been asked to fish along the way.

The "catch" is often a quiet sort of thing. It may take time. A sudden pull on the net and the fish swim away.

You have made a difference in people's lives. If you have wanted to know all those times, then now you need to know that you cannot know. It is for *the* Fisherman to know, not you.

Following him is the most important thing you could have done. You need to believe that. It is true.

If you had not left your "other nets" behind, something

would not have happened in the kingdom of God. It is that simple. You were needed. You *are* needed. That is why he called you.

It is now time for you to gently step toward another boat, another day of fishing, another time filled with mystery. The One who called you wants you to know that he is still calling. Hearing his call is a matter of trust, not certainty.

There have been times when you have slipped through his net. You have wanted freedom from his yoke. There have been times when the promised light burden felt heavy. He knows of those times. He understands. He has listened to your request for healing.

And so the net slips around you again. Feel its pull. Experience its embrace.

There is still much to do. Listen. Again he says, "Follow me." It is time to begin again, but this time you have remembered that first time he called to you. You have looked back at those places of origin. You have confessed to him about those moments when you tried to escape his grasp. You have complained, offered honest resistance, and asked for the grace of healing.

Reach out to his reaching out to you. You are a child of God. You are loved. You are one of his wounded ministers.

It is time for healing.

Conclusion

Those of us in ministry are living out a story. We are familiar with another story that has helped define who we are. This other story speaks of naked children who would not listen to limits, brothers who fell victim to ambition, kings who forgot that God was sovereign, prophets who burned up their souls in doing the Lord's work, women who courageously cut a path of faith in uncharted lands, and disciples who learned that the initial enthusiasm for following Jesus was not going to be enough for the long haul.

We know that story, but we have forgotten that it reflects our stories. We need to remember how powerful the biblical story is, not just for those to whom we minister, but how powerful it is to us. The biblical story gives shape to our shadows. The narrative of those in the past sheds light on that which we often try to hide.

Like those first two youths in the garden, we do not stay healthy when we hide. Healing cannot be ours as long as we proclaim that there is no problem.

As I write these words, there are a number of my colleagues who have "fallen on their own swords." They are not to be considered blameless nor are they to escape accountability. The ministry should expect those in its number to struggle to maintain high moral and professional standards. But it is time to recognize the high-risk nature of our work. It is time to name the demons so that they will not have power over us.

It is time to put aside the judgmental atmosphere that seems so prevalent in the gathering of the faithful, so that we can make prominent some questions concerning the reasons there are so many wounded among us. Some of the answers begin in the story that called us into being.

This book began with reflections about the perils of ministry in light of some biblical models. We have much new learning to do from some very old stories. This learning must begin with an honest appraisal of who we are as human beings who were called into ministry. To bypass who we are plants seeds of trouble for later work. The reason I believe so much in an instrument like the Enneagram is that it allows the observer to discover the roots of why he or she became the kind of person he or she has become. Many clergy are projecting a personal agenda onto their ministry without being aware of what they are doing. Blame, hurt, and anger are the results of such denial of unique human characteristics and individual wounds from the past.

The Enneagram helps a person name his or her soul. What a marvelous place to begin anew the journey of examining why we do what we do. It is time to grow up. It is time to quit blaming the church for all of our pain. The church is surely the reason for some of our pain, but the roots lie in our reaction to "mother" church.

So many of the games we play in ministry come from unmet ego needs. It is time to throw the ego up on the screen to see what hides under our robes and roles. We need to both weep and laugh about many of the things we do as ministers. "The emperor is naked". . . and we are the emperors.

The twenty-one-day spiritual journey is a representative way of stating that we need to be pilgrims on the journey rather than observers or tourists. How can we lead others on spiritual paths if we are not first led? We have so much to learn from a reexamination of our own stories.

My own pain led me to sharing these words with you. The attempt to do God's work has been the most rewarding and the most tiresome thing I have ever tried. The expectations of us held by the people we serve are sometimes comical. We know that, and yet we often try to meet many of those expectations. Why?

If we give control to the people we serve, we will be like a top that gains its direction by the pull of so many strings. We need to stop the top and look at its shape while it is at rest.

Much of what we do in ministry is because of who we are or who we wish we were. We need to claim our mixed motives. We do not have to stand naked in some pulpit and explain the complexities of why we are in ministry, but somewhere, sometime we need to spend time at the spring drinking some water.

Ministers need to care more for the wounded in our number. It could be us. In many ways "they" are us, and we fear their wounds, for they are potential scars that could be on our own souls.

We do not need to care for one another because of some deep, psychological truth that has been discovered about the hidden motives of ministers. We need to care for one another because the Shepherd of the sheep calls us to be wounded healers and spiritual directors who know the need to be led.

We ministers need to care for our own souls as though they are sacred items rather than what we get around to after we have done our religious work. The price is too high for neglecting the soul.

It is a time for healing. I rejoice in what I see happening in the ministry. The pain is coming out, and it scares both clergy and laity. Good. We need to be scared. We need to have our attention gained. We need to acknowledge and accept our humanness. The work of the soul is demanding attention. The gospel of Christ challenges the local shepherds to not only tend to the sheep but to care for the shepherds.

It is time for healing. Thanks be to God.

Notes

Introduction

1. John A. Sanford, *Ministry Burnout* (Louisville: Westminster/John Knox Press, 1982), 48.

Part I

Adam and Eve

1. Allen Nauss, "The Ministerial Personality: Myth or Reality," *Journal of Religion and Health* 12 (1973), 77-95.

2. Alan Jones, *Sacrifice and Delight: Spirituality for Ministry* (New York: HarperCollins, 1992), 40.

3. John A. Sanford, *Ministry Burnout* (Louisville: Westminster/John Knox Press, 1982), 45.

4. Joseph Campbell, *The Power of Myth* (New York: Doubleday, 1988).

5. Eugene H. Peterson, *Under the Unpredictable Plant: An Exploration in Vocational Holiness* (Grand Rapids, Mich.: Wm. B. Eerdmans Publishing, Co., 1992), 112-113.

6. Jones, 2.

Cain and Abel

1. Thomas Maeder, "Wounded Healers," *The Atlantic Monthly*, January 1989, 40-41.

2. Eugene H. Peterson, *Under the Unpredictable Plant: An Exploration in Vocational Holiness* (Grand Rapids, Mich.: Wm. B.

Eerdmans Publishing, Co., 1992), 14.

3. H. Newton Maloney and Richard A. Hunt, *The Psychology of Clergy* (Harrisburg, Pa.: Morehouse Publishing, 1991), 119.

4. Alan Jones, *Sacrifice and Delight: Spirituality for Ministry* (New York: HarperCollins, 1992), 25.

Jacob and Esau

1. H. Newton Maloney and Richard A. Hunt, *The Psychology of Clergy* (Harrisburg, Pa.: Morehouse Publishing, 1991), 11-21.

2. John A. Sanford, *Ministry Burnout* (Louisville: Westminster/John Knox Press, 1982), 14.

3. Ursula K. Le Guin, *A Wizard of Earthsea* (New York, Macmillan, 1968).

4. Alan Jones, *Sacrifice and Delight: Spirituality for Ministry* (New York: HarperCollins, 1992), 31.

Saul

1. Norman Shawchuck and Roger Heuser, *Leading the Congregation: Caring for Yourself While Serving Others* (Nashville: Abingdon, 1993), 66.

2. John A. Sanford, *Ministry Burnout* (Louisville: Westminster/John Knox Press, 1982), 76-77.

3. All Scripture references in Part I are from the Revised Standard Version of the Bible.

4. H. Newton Maloney and Richard A. Hunt, *The Psychology of Clergy* (Harrisburg, Pa.: Morehouse Publishing, 1991), 36.

5. Eugene H. Peterson, *Working the Angles: The Shape of Pastoral Integrity* (Grand Rapids, Mich.: Wm. B. Eerdmans Publishing, Co., 1987), 168-169.

David

1. Richard A. Blackmon, "The Hazards of Ministry" (Ph.D diss., Graduate School of Psychology, Fuller Theological Seminary, 1984), quoted in Maloney and Hunt, 35.

2. Maloney and Hunt, *The Psychology of Clergy*, 36.

3. Alan Jones, *Sacrifice and Delight: Spirituality for Ministry* (New York: HarperCollins, 1992), 11-12.

4. Ibid., 44.

5. Urban T. Holmes, *Spirituality for Ministry* (San Francisco: Harper & Row, 1982), 42-43.

6. Jones, 53-54.

Jeremiah

1. H. Newton Maloney and Richard A. Hunt, *The Psychology of Clergy* (Harrisburg, Pa.: Morehouse Publishing, 1991), 145.
2. Ibid.
3. John A. Sanford, *Ministry Burnout* (Louisville: Westminster/John Knox Press, 1982), 5-16.
4. Ibid., 103-114.

Esther

1. Judy Rosener, "Ways Women Lead," *Harvard Business Review* (November/December 1990), 120.
2. Norman Shawchuck and Roger Heuser, *Leading the Congregation: Caring for Yourself While Serving Others* (Nashville: Abingdon, 1993), 253-276.
3. Edward C. Lehman, Jr., *Women Clergy: Breaking through Gender Barriers* (New Brunswick, N.J.: Transaction Books, 1985), 190.
4. Ibid.
5. Jackson W. Carroll, Barbara Hargrove, and Adair T. Lummis, *Women of the Cloth* (San Francisco: Harper & Row, 1981), 208.
6. H. Newton Maloney and Richard A. Hunt, *The Psychology of Clergy* (Harrisburg, Pa.: Morehouse Publishing, 1991), 43-53.
7. Some of the comments I have offered about women can also relate to African American clergy who serve in predominantly white denominations. In retreats I have led in the area of clergy renewal, I have listened to the pain of some of these black pastors who feel they have nowhere to go in a closed system that is not open to "any person as pastor."

The white church must grapple with what it means to be open. It appears to me that the white church, for the most part, does not desire this kind of openness. The result is pain when we keep talking about the possibility of sending any pastor to any church when it is not a reality. I speak from my view as a United Methodist pastor in a system of "sent" ministry.

Simon Peter

1. Norman Shawchuck and Roger Heuser, *Leading the Congregation: Caring for Yourself While Serving Others* (Nashville:

Abingdon, 1993), 79.

2. Ibid., 87-88.

3. Eugene H. Peterson, *Under the Unpredictable Plant: An Exploration in Vocational Holiness* (Grand Rapids, Mich.: Wm. B. Eerdmans Publishing, Co., 1992), 60.

4. Ibid., 80-81.

5. H. Newton Maloney and Richard A. Hunt, *The Psychology of Clergy* (Harrisburg, Pa.: Morehouse Publishing, 1991), 113.

6. Ibid., 113-120.

Part II

Explanation of the Enneagram

1. John A. Sanford, *Ministry Burnout* (Louisville: Westminster/John Knox Press, 1982), 70-71.

The Nine Types

1. Richard Rohr and Andreas Ebert, *Discovering the Enneagram: An Ancient Tool for a New Spiritual Journey* (New York: Crossroad, 1990).

Part III

Spiritual Renewal Journey

1. All Scripture references in Part III are from the New Revised Standard Version of the Bible.